THE EFFECTS-BASED BOARD:

AN EFFECTS-BASED APPROACH TO THE JOINT OPERATIONS PLANNING PROCESS

COLIN BEATTY MARCUM

DEPARTMENT OF THE ARMY
G 3/5/7, U.S. ARMY FIRES CENTER OF EXCELLENCE AND FORT SILL
FORT SILL, OKLAHOMA 73503-5100

ATZR-CO   28 August 2014

MEMORANDUM FOR RECORD

SUBJECT: The Effects based Board: An effects-Based Approach to the Joint Opperations Planning Process.
A thesis by CPT Colin Marcum for American Military University

1. The required Antiterorism/OPSEC review was conducted for the The Effects based Board

2. Quite simply, while this is a very thorough paper, it lacks any specificity that would make for any knid of AT or OPSEC violation. The only real discussion that specificially adresses names, locations or tactics are those of a historical nature.

3. **Antiterrorism/OPSEC Review Signature:** I am ATO level II certified and have reviewed the requirements package and understand my responsibilities IAW AR 525-13, Antiterrorism and AR 530-1, OPSEC.

4. POC for this memorandum is SFC Perry, at 580-558-0948.

CHRISTOPHER P. PERRY
SFC, USA
G3, AT/OPSEC OFFICER

This publication is a for commercial publication version of the author's Master's Thesis in partial degree fulfillment of a Master of Arts in Military Studies from the American Military University, part of the American Public University System on August 27, 2014.

DEDICATION

I dedicate this published work to my wife, Hillma, and daughter, Ellie, whose support and patience was crucial to completing this thesis.

TABLE OF CONTENTS

TABLE OF FIGURES

ACKNOWLEDGMENTS

I would like to acknowledge the guidance provided by my thesis professor, David Woodworth, and the instructors from the Department of Military Studies of the American Military University.

I would like to thank the assistance of my colleagues at the Fires Center of Excellence and Fort Sill, Mr. Darrell Ames for reviewing my work, and for SFC Christopher Perry for clearing it through OPSEC.

Finally, the artwork produced by Danny Huynh added significant value to this finished product.

I
INTRODUCTION

"Warfare is the greatest affair of state, the basis of life and death, the Way to survival or extinction. It must be thoroughly pondered and analyzed." –Sun Tzu[1]

When the leaders of the Armed Forces of the United States conduct deliberate or crisis action planning they utilize the Joint Operations Planning Process (JOPP). The JOPP is a seven step tool for developing operations orders in support of the joint force commander's (JFC) desired end-state. When the process is initiated proactively; deliberate planning, or reactively; crisis action planning, the staff of the JFC begin course of action (COA) development based on national objectives, joint force assets, and the commander's intent. Once a variety of COAs have been properly wargamed and compared then the JFC approves a single COA to follow, and the staff begins work on order development and publication. It is a functional process by which the joint force can conduct operations based on a specific operational environment; however, there is a negative attribute to this method.

The most critical flaw of the JOPP is that the orders produced on a selected COA developed during the process may not actually bring about the desired end-state. For every event there is a cause,

[1] Sawyer, Ralph D. *Sun Tzu: Art of War* (Boulder, CO; Westview Press. 1994), 167

and a desired end-state is merely a culmination of the effects of a number of causes. Within the operational environment there are numerous conditions which are interrelated to each other to varying degrees. An effect created by a single action on one of those variables will not only have direct implications, but may themselves become the causes of other effects; these are termed second and third-order (STO) effects. When STO effects are not accounted for during the planning process then even if the initial intended effect for a COA supports the conditions necessary for the desired end-state their subsequent effects may negatively impact the effort and thus fail to achieve that end-state. During the *mission analysis* step of the JOPP reviewing forces allocated to the joint force can come prior to determining mission success criteria. The means of the joint force can be identified to the staff before they even determine what it is they must accomplish in order to become successful. As a result, during COA development they will inherently focus on shaping the COA and its effects based on what assets are available instead of determining what effects they need to create to support the desired end-state and then tailoring the force to achieve those effects.

This comes about due to military planners placing emphasis on military means in order to create desired effects. Without knowledge of the non-military conditions of the operational environment then planners will naturally fall upon what they know best; (e.g. military matters).This is detrimental to the desired end-state because the conditions of the operational environment have unique and complex relationships that change the nature of effects as they cascade throughout that environment creating unintended or undesired STO effects.

Developing COAs that create effects necessary to bring about the desired end-state is naturally what we should be striving to achieve, but that raises the question. **How do we change the current planning process in order to develop COAs that achieve the desired end-state within such complex operational environments?**

Hypothesis

The effects-based approach (EBA) is a concept which drives the development of COAs based on effects that need to be achieved instead of the means available. Based on the required conditions that need to be shaped in order to bring about a desired end-state, the EBA determines what effects are necessary in order to establish those conditions. Planners then pair the desired effects with the various systems and tools available that can deliver those effects. The STO effects created after the utilization of various means are compared and contrasted. Positive STO effects are maintained while negative ones are mitigated or otherwise may require reassessment of the delivery platform or the desired effect itself. EBA is inherently supportive of the desired end-state, because it seeks to create the conditions necessary to bring it about. In order to achieve the level of understanding necessary to effectively utilize EBA we need a board of personnel whose combined knowledge encompasses the entire breadth of the operational environment. Their shared understanding will provide clarity on the nature of conditions and relationships within that environment and aid in COA development. Through the adaptation of the current JOPP to incorporate methods more in-line with the process of the EBA the joint force can produce deliberate and crisis action plans that achieve the desired end-state.

The purpose of this research is to support the nation's interests through the improvement of our current JOPP in order to increase joint operation success, and more importantly ensure that success is nested with our national objectives. Our joint forces are very competent in their execution of military operations, and their ability to achieve military objectives. The point of military operations; however, is that they support the political objectives of the nation, and we have seen the ramification of failing to nest military objectives with political ones. The armed forces of the United States and its partners achieved military victories in Vietnam, but they suffered from a lack of an overarching political objective. After completion of the combat phases of Operation Enduring Freedom and Operation Iraqi Freedom we saw our military forces having to cope with combating insurgents and foreign fighters for over a decade. One of the reasons for the rise of the insurgency in Iraq can be attributed to the dissolution of the Iraqi defense apparatus put into motion by Coalition Provisional Authority Order Number 2.[2] The reabsorption of these combatants back into civilian society and the collapse of public services led many into the fledgling insurgency to which combat planners did not anticipate. By understanding the nature of effects within the operational environment, guided by principles of EBA, and a board of experts, whose knowledge of the operational environment help COA development, we can develop plans that account and shape all conditions necessary for the desired end-state.

---

[2] Coalition Provisional Authority, *Coalition Provisional Authority Order Number 2.* Accessed August 02, 2014. http://www.casi.org.uk/info/cpa/030523-CPA-Order2.pdf

II
LITERATURE REVIEW

All sectors of government affairs are important for the functioning of a nation, but the importance of conflict to the conduct of the state cannot be understated. Economic and social policies over the centuries have had a considerable impact on the undertaking of countries, but often that impact is created slowly over time; taking years or decades to reach full effect. War and military operations other than war (MOOTW), conversely, can create greater, sweeping effects in a shorter amount of time when compared to other matters of state. Rome may not have been built in a day, but it can – and has – been destroyed in as short a timeframe. Empires, nations, and city-states take decades and centuries to rise into greatness through successful military campaigns, foreign diplomacy, and internal development, but the failure of a single strategic objective of a campaign can delegitimize their authority and prestige. If a nation seeks to sustain itself then it is of the upmost importance to determine how to develop sound campaign plans that achieve those objectives.

This importance is not lost on contemporary military planners. In an attempt to further understand the complexities of planning for military operations in diverse operational environments the EBA provides a solution. The premise of EBA is that by focusing on the effects required to set conditions necessary for the desired end-state we empower our military forces with the methods necessary to achieve greater results with less overall effort.[3] Whereas the older attrition-based approach focused on generally conventional military means to sap the strength of an enemy's ability to resist overtime, the EBA allows for greater involvement of other non-military means. Through an understanding of how effects are created, how they change based on variables within the operational environment, and how they can create STO effects, either intentionally or not, we can develop COAs that support the desired end-state. But before we can delve deeper into discussion on how exactly EBA and assessments of the operational environment can shape COAs we need to define a few terms.

Edward Smith from the Department of Defense's Command and Control Research Program referenced some of the confusion based around the term *effect*. In his book *Effects-Based Operations: Applying Network Centric Warfare in Peace, Crisis, and War* he stated that, "The term *effect* has been routinely used in military writings to imply everything from outcomes or results, to operational objectives, to the blast radius of a weapon's warhead."[4] In attrition-based warfare, the view that effects are predominantly kinetic or non-kinetic in nature resulting from the use of lethal and non-lethal systems has slowly begun to lose favor. Within the targeting community, effects are viewed in relation to the impact that an action has on the capabilities and functions of an enemy system. Furthermore, the effect does not necessarily require a military asset to create, but instead these effects contributing to military operations can come from non-military sources.[5]

For Smith's writing he decided to refer to effects in their generalized term, and that "An effect is a result of impact created by application of military or other power."[6] Basically, this means that

[3] Deptula, David A. BG (USAF). *Effects-Based Operations: Change in the Nature of Warfare* (Arlington, VA; Aerospace Education Foundation, 2001) 11

[4] Smith, Edward A. *Effects Based Operations: Applying Network Centric Warfare in Peace, Crisis, and War* (Washington, D.C.; CCRP Press, 2002) 110

[5] Smith, 110-111

anything can create an effect. Establishing coalitions, empowering international media, dropping bombs, and enacting sanctions are examples of the four elements of national power: diplomatic, informational, military, and economic (DIME), and under this definition these sources of national strength become viable capabilities to delivering effects. With a diverse array of military and non-military assets that can be utilized to achieve similar or complementary effects planners can begin assessment on what forces and resources are necessary to set the conditions for the desired end-state.

Now that we have come to a common definition of effects what is their role in EBA? The joint force's Commander's Handbook for an Effects-Based Approach to Joint Operations states that, "An effects-based approach to joint operations focuses on improving our ability to affect an adversary's behavior and/or capabilities through the integrated application of select instruments of national power."[7] From this statement we can determine that the purpose of effects within the EBA is not only to affect the will or degrade the capabilities of the enemy, but that the effect delivered is only one amongst a series of other effects that have been planned and coordinated to complement each other for a compounding effect.

The perception amongst proponents of EBA is that this approach offers planners a way to achieve more with less effort. Lieutenant General David A. Deptula was a member of the *Black Hole* cell which was tasked with planning the first night operation of Operation Desert Storm. In order for the following air campaign against Iraq to succeed they needed to cripple Saddam Hussein's Integrated Air Defense Systems (IADS) and Command and Control (C2) apparatuses. The plan they developed sought not to destroy those systems, but instead neutralize their ability to function. Dropping a single bomb upon an IADS's radar meant that the entire

---

[6] Smith, 111

[7] Joint Warfighting Center. *Commander's Handbook for an Effects-Based Approach to Joint Operations* (Washington, D.C.; Government Printing Office, 2006) I-1

system was removed from the fight, because its surface to air missile launchers would not be able to target friendly aircraft. Similarly, a single bomb dropped on the wing of a C2 structure generally resulted in the entire structure's personnel being evacuated which neutralized that target.[8] Though the plan didn't call for complete target destruction, *Black Hole*'s plan was able to achieve the same effect; degrading and defeating the enemy's capability to resist. Since they didn't need to commit greater resources to completely destroying these systems this permitted them to redirect now excess resources to the next set of priority targets. "Force used to effectively control a system – to achieve specific effects rather than destroy it – may lead to the same strategically relevant result, yet with significantly less force."[9] As effects-based thinking had begun to permeate throughout the joint force two concepts were developed in order to help make it work at the operational level of war.

The first was the systems-of-systems analysis (SOSA) which is, "an analytical process that holistically examines a potential adversary and/or operational environment as a complex, adaptive system, including its structures, behavior, and capabilities in order to identify and assess critical factors and system interrelationships."[10] SOSA seeks to take something that is inherently very complex, like the inner-workings of a nation, and visualize all the elements of that system upon a web to determine how and where functions and capabilities are connected. For example, the health and wellbeing of non-combatant populations are directly connected to various institutions; i.e. schools, hospitals, fire houses, police stations, markets, and power stations. They are in turn connected to each other and other sectors of the nation, like the personnel that are affiliated with those areas, as well as, other sectors and their personnel, like government buildings, military installations, ports, airfields, and industrial facilities. Upon completion of this

---

[8] Deptula, 14-15
[9] Deptula, 6
[10] Joint Warfighting Center, GL-8

interconnected web planners can identify key nodes within the system and determine where best to apply effects in order to exploit that system.

The second element is the Operational Net Assessment (ONA) which "develops a pre-crisis knowledge base of the adversary's systems and capabilities for the creation of ONA… [It] becomes a repository for theater perspective and knowledge of the Commander's area of responsibility, key issues, and regional players."[11] ONA provides joint staff planners a baseline for understanding how the enemy's systems function, and assist in the creation of SOSA diagrams. Due to the ONA permitting a more in-depth look into the operational environment it also assists national planners in developing objectives for support of national interests during times of peace and lead ups towards war.

The most difficult requisite of EBA comes from accurate analysis of the operational environment in which military operations will be conducted, which is needed for SOSA and ONA development. The variables that exist within this environment are able to change the nature of effects produced by a coordinated action, and thus any COA developed needs to take into account these variables. Inherently all effects created should be geared towards getting us closer to the conditions necessary to achieve our desired end-state, but the presence of an unaccounted variable can change the dynamics of the operation. Intended actions can then produce an effect that is counter-productive to our overall intent. This generally comes in the form of STO effects which are the effects produced as a result of other effects. For example, destroying a power station can create a first-order effect of denying electricity to an area, and the potential second-order effect produced could be loss of life support systems at a hospital in that area. This can lead into the third-order effect of loss of non-combatant life and loss in confidence in friendly

---

[11] Hannan, Michael J. LCDR (USN). Operational Net Assessment: A Framework for Social Network Analysis. Accessed May 18, 2014. (http://www.au.af.mil/info-ops/iosphere/iosphere_fall05_hannan.pdf) 27

forces or local government.

The consensus amongst people like Smith and Deptula is that the ability for EBA to leverage the diverse portfolio of military and non-military means available to the government is inherently beneficial, because it opens up multiple avenues for achieving the same desired end-state. It allows for *A Whole of Government Approach* to defense interests which are in line with President Barrack Obama's *National Security Strategy* for 2010.

> *We are improving the integration of skills and capabilities within our military and civilian institutions, so they complement each other and operate seamlessly. We are also improving coordinated planning and policymaking and must build our capacity in key areas where we fall short. This requires close cooperation with Congress and a deliberate and inclusive interagency process, so that we achieve integration of our efforts to implement and monitor operations, policies, and strategies.*[12]

President Obama's intent was to reduce the nation's overreliance on our military to support our national interests, and with his *Whole of Government Approach* he set the challenge for the government to unify its efforts. Beyond just the military aspect of national power a government can leverage its intelligence agencies to help develop an assessment of the operational environment: enemy military forces, political hierarchies, critical social functions and vulnerabilities, and other variables. With its emphasis on effects rather than means EBA seems to be most supportive of the President's intent, however, others have identified problems within the approach.

As a result, EBA is not without its detractors. In 2008, General James N. Mattis of the United States Marine Corps was the Commanding General of United States Joint Force Command (USJFCOM) and wrote to *Joint Force Quarterly* of his impressions of effects-based operations (EBO). He stated in his article "USFCOM Commander's Guidance for Effects-Based Operations" that, "after a

---

[12] Obama, Barack H. *National Security Strategy* (Washington, D.C.; Government Printing Office, 2010) 14

thorough evaluation it is my assessment that the ideas reflected in EBO, ONA, and SOSA have not delivered on their advertised benefits and that a clear understanding of these concepts has proven problematic and elusive for U.S. and multinational personnel." He believed that EBA had too many flaws to make it a viable planning process. He thought that regardless of the resources available that the approach required an "unachievable level of predictability" and an unrealistic assessment of the operational environment. COAs developed through EBA would require such intricate detail that it would hinder effective reaction to unforeseen and inevitable changes on the battlefield, and that overall the approach was too confusing to execute reliably; especially amongst junior officer and multinational partners.[13]

Mattis references the failure of Israeli Defense Force (IDF) to properly execute EBA during its conflict with Hezbollah in 2006. Matt Matthews wrote for Combat Studies Institute on this conflict, and shared his assessment of the IDF's failures with EBA and its elements.

> *The Effects-Based Operations (EBO) and Systemic Operational Design-inspired doctrine that vigorously embraced air power at the expense of a classic ground maneuver campaign was certainly a major factor in the IDF's disappointing performance... As enemy rockets rained down on northern Israel, the IDF attempted to orchestrate the strategic cognitive collapse of Hezbollah through the use of air power and precision firepower-based operations. When this failed, the IDF sought to produce the same effects by using its ground forces to conduct limited raids and probes into southern Lebanon. These restrained initiatives designed to create a cognitive perception of defeat also failed to produce the effects necessary to incapacitate Hezbollah.[14]*

---

[13] Mattis, James N. GEN (USMC) "USJFCOM Commander's Guidance for Effects-based Operations." *Joint Forces Quarterly* (Washington, D.C.; NDU Press, issue 51, 4th quarter 2008) 106

[14] Matthews, Matt M. *We Were Caught Unprepared: The 2006 Hezbollah-Israeli War* (Fort Leavenworth, KS; Combat Studies Institute Press, 2008) 61

The failure of the IDF to create the effects they were trying to achieve resulted in wide-spread criticism of the concept of the EBA to support deliberate and crisis-action COA development. Zoltan Jobbagy in his article "Effects-based Operations and the Problem of Causality" touched on this issue when he stated, "an effects-based approach is generally good for creating desired physical effects and might occasionally be good for generating desired systemic effects. However, in the case of psychological effects, the best we can say is that the concept does not work well."[15] He believed this because he viewed psychological connections, between the various entities within the operational environment, as too complex to properly identify and assess the nature of their "linkages."[16]

The problem of operationalizing EBO, however, was not that it demanded an unrealistic level of understating of the operational environment, but that it was never designed to be operationalized in the first place. John T. Correl, former editor of AIR FORCE magazine, wrote that when JFCOM developed the SOSA and ONA to bring EBO to the operational level of war that it inherently created the problems that its detractors identify as being a failure. In referencing a comment made by former United States Marine Corps Commandant Lieutenant General Paul Van Riper, "Deptula and [Colonel John Warden] were right when they 'demanded that targeting officers expand their horizons and determine how best to attack systems rather than targets' and that it was the JFCOM variant of EBO that 'most damaged operational thinking.'"[17] In other words, under our current capabilities effects-based concepts should only be utilized to develop strategic level guidance, not operational level.

While opponents of the EBA have rational critiques there is an issue to their argument. They conclude that because the joint force

---

[15] Jobbagy, Zoltan. "Effects-based Operations and the Problem of Causality." *Joint Forces Quarterly* (Washington, D.C.; NDU Press, issue 46, 3rd quarter 2007) 93
[16] Jobbagy, 91
[17] Correll, John T. "The Assault on EBO." *AIR FORCE Magazine* (Arlington, VA; Air Force Association, January 2013) 54

lacks the ability to fully understand the nature of the operational environment, like General Mattis surmised, or that it simply fails to achieve the desired effects, like the IDF attempted, that the EBA is inherently a faulty concept. Is the lack of complete understanding of the operational environment a fault of the EBA concept or of the apparatuses available to the joint force to fully assess that environment? If joint force planners had access to the necessary resources, or if current intelligence capabilities were optimized to have near complete understanding of all the variables within the operational environment, would plans developed through this approach still be faulty? Could the failure of plans developed through EBA fall with the planners improperly following the effects-based process? The plan the IDF used was highly influenced by the United States' COA to defeat the Iraqi Armed Forces in 1991 and 2003. However, who would presume that duplicating a concept developed to defeat the Iraqis would still be applicable to Hezbollah?

Like all COAs dealing with shaping the operational environment, in order to achieve the desired end-state it appears the biggest issue needing to be resolved is having a way in which to achieve a high degree of understanding of that environment. If there was an apparatus available that could achieve such a level of clarity could the desired end-state be achieved? This thesis will seek to address this issue, and provide solutions to the problems previously stated.

III
UNIVERSAL CONDITIONS

Within an operational environment, there are conditions that exist which influence the nature of warfare. They affect how COAs are executed, how objectives are achieved, and the way in which effects are delivered and observed. Every operational environment is under the influence of these universal conditions, but the nature of them differ in complexity and degree to such a point that even if an organization conducted the same action in two separate operational environments then their effects would differ. Ultimately, these conditions determine whether actions taken create the effects necessary to achieve the desired end-state.

What we are attempting to create through the analysis of the conditions present within the operational environment is one or more COAs that are capable of shaping those conditions to achieve the desired end-state. In a mathematical sense, all COAs are dependant variables because their design is dependent on the conditions of the operational environment, which act as independent variables.[18] The differences in how governments and their militaries plan for operations are simply variations in how to analyze, assess, and incorporate their understanding of those conditions into

---

[18] Cambridge Dictionary, "Dependent Variables," Accessed 19 June 2014 http://dictionary.cambridge.org/us/dictionary/british/dependent-variable.

actionable COAs.

With EBA's emphasis on prior knowledge of the operational environment, and currency of their situational understanding, its planners are better able to produce plans designed achieve the desired end-state, because the focus of its efforts is on associating actions with the desired behavioral responses. Edward Smith mentioned that through EBA planners could handle the complex nature of these independent variables by, "orchestrating the right actions to create the behavioral effects we want to produce; determining which cascades of direct and indirect effects are likely to stem from our actions; and determining which effects we have actually created."[19]

Smith further explained that because the nature of the conditions of the operational environment are so complex, as to be too difficult to understand in its entirety, that COAs developed through EBA needed to focus on accuracy of behavioral response, instead of the exactness of them. In describing the successful implementation of EBA throughout history, "They bounded the complexity by looking at and choosing certain kinds of actions that were likely to produce certain kinds of effects so as to find a workable answer."[20] This allows for more variance in the effects produced, and during COA development, the incorporation of variance allows for more flexibility towards follow on actions. Exactness in those non-physical effects is near impossible to achieve, but accuracy in those effects is more manageable. Hence, a COA built on exactness is more apt to failure, because it lacks the flexibility required in an operational environment that is impossible to fathom in its entirety. Establishing flexible, but accurate, effect requirements leads to COAs that progress towards the desired end-state in a *workable* manner. The question that is raised is what exactly are the conditions to which we speak, and how do they affect the direction COAs take?

To answer this question requires an understanding of two separate concepts that come together within the operational environment.

---

[19] Smith, 231
[20] Smith, 233

First is the systems perspective, in which the operational environment is perceived as a system of systems. By joint definition, a systems perspective, "strives to provide an understanding of significant relationships within interrelated PMESII [political, military, economic, social, informational, and infrastructural] and other systems relevant to a specific joint operation, without regard to geographic boundaries."[21] By bounding sectors; like military, economic, social, and others, then determining their critical components, and indentifying linkages in those components internally and into other sectors, planners can identify strengths and weakness within the systems.

The second concept is that of causation, which for every effect, there are one or more interrelated causes, and for every cause, there is a creation of one or more effects, which in turn, can be the causes of further effects, also known as STO effects. This means that any element within the operational environment has the capability to change the dynamics of cause and effect relationships. Particular conditions within the operational environment, like economic strength, can be directly affected by the condition of other sectors (e.g. industry and commerce), as well as experience a STO effect indirectly from others (e.g. agriculture and human services). When one looks at causation, and understands how linkages between the conditions of the operational environment and a single action, either physical or psychological, can create a cascade of effects throughout a system, then planners can exploit it to their benefit.[22]

Imagine that a COA calls for projection of power in order to control key cities along a coastline, and planners determined that this would best be accomplished via an amphibious landing of United States Marines onto the beaches of that coast. A key element of that plan for a successful landing is the offloading of M1A2 Abrams main battle tanks in order to provide armored maneuver firepower to the

---

[21] Joint Staff, *Joint Publication 2-01.3: Joint Intelligence Preparation of the Operational Environment* (Washington, D.C.; Government Printing Office, 2009) I-3
[22] Smith, 319-320

infantry pushing inland. Without that armored support the infantry may find it difficult if not impossible to maneuver towards their objectives. Something as simple as the consistency of the sand and soil along the beaches, may bog down those multi-ton vehicles, and make them susceptible to rocket and artillery fire. In this case, the condition of the terrain of that particular area of the operational environment could be a critical flaw in the course of operations unless properly assessed. Seeing that something as simple as the condition of the beaches can affect the outcome of operations we will now identify all the conditions present within the operational environment.

Desired End-State

Determining the desired end-state is placed first on the list of independent variables, because it is the most important. Not only do all operations revolve around it, but it determines the conditions by which all efforts are designed to achieve. "Planning begins with the end state in mind, providing a unifying purpose around which actions and resources are focused."[23] Without a definitive desired end-state no detailed plan can be developed. Forces cannot be tailored, resources allocated, and movement made without it, and thus must be determined as soon as possible to avoid time critical delays. A tentative desired end-state can be established with available information in order to allow planning to begin taking place; however, a definitive end-state must be made before COAs are fully developed. This is because changes between the tentative and definitive desired end-state can have tremendous implications on any planning that has already been conducted.

In most publications the term *end state* is defined in the same manner that *desired end-state* is in this thesis. For example in *Joint Publication 1-02: Department of Defense Dictionary of Military and Associated Terms* defined *end state* as, "The set of required conditions that defines

---

[23] Joint Staff, *Joint Publication 1: Doctrine for the Armed Forces of the United States* (Washington, D.C.; Government Printing Office, 2013), I-19

achievement of the commander's objectives."[24] The reason for the propensity of use of the term *desired end-state* over just *end state* comes from perspective that this paper has towards causality. By the conclusion of operations, either conditions will be what were desired or not, and thus an end state will exist even if it was not what the commander intended. Imagine the end state of Vietnam after the fall of Saigon. The whole of the country was under communist control, which became the end state though, not the desired end state.

The desired end-state is not just about imposing our will upon an enemy combatant, but about shaping all variables within the operational environment to create those conditions necessary to bring it about. There is little benefit towards defeating an adversary if the result is not in line with the desired end-state. Beyond the conditions of the enemy, other interrelated conditions affect actions within the operational environment. Understanding the desired end-state will help in determining what the conditions need to be by close of operation, and will, as a result, drive the COA development process and the employment of ways and means to shape those conditions. The sections following this will describe in detail the nature of those conditions, but it is important to understand that the end state is in relation to the conditions of the operational environment, and to bring about that desired end-state means shaping those conditions to match.

It is imperative that the desired end-state guide the development of COAs, and that in doing so, all conditions are given equal importance. Failure to properly anticipate the nature of conditions may produce undesired or collateral effects when actions are employed. These effects, either physical or behavioral, can produce a cascade of effects that invariably alter the conditions of the operational environment in a direction away from what is required for the desired end-state. A good example of when planners failed to properly account for all the conditions of the operational

---

[24] Joint Staff, *Joint Publication 1-02: Department of Defense Dictionary of Military and Associated Terms* (Washington, D.C.; Government Printing Office, 2014) 87

environment can be seen during the 2003 invasion of Iraq; Operation Iraqi Freedom (OIF). The United States focused heavily on the enemy conditions within the operational environment, but much of their presumptions were based on their experiences during Desert Storm. They anticipated the Iraqi armed forces might use various methods to counter the coalition advance, from the use of biological or chemical weapons to ecological sabotage of their own oil fields. Additionally, the United States planned for a flood of refugees by bolstering supplies of food and water for that contingency. What actually transpired was a guerrilla war, as former Iraqi armed forces personnel threw down their arms and blended back into civilian communities, becoming the first wave of insurgents to fight against coalition supply lines.

Most knowledgeable observers assume that, barring the use of unconventional weapons, such would be the result; the Iraqi military, demoralized, ill-equipped, and psychologically overawed by the superpower whose forces had crushed them a decade before, could not be expected to put up much of a fight. But what happened next was a surprise. An insurgency began, not acknowledged as such by American leaders for a good half year after the overthrow of the regime.[25]

Additionally, the collapse of many of the basic public services (e.g. schools, hospitals, power stations) followed in the wake of the coalition advance caused an increase in the level of disturbance amongst the civilian population. When military planners acknowledged the insurgent threat, and conducted counterinsurgency operations to attempt to defeat it, there was still a level of separation between military and civilian efforts. As noted by Eliot Cohen and John Gooch, "All successful counterinsurgencies require a blending of civilian and military measures; such wars are about security, to be sure, but also about the provision of electrical power, jobs, and the basic requirements of a decent life such as sewage treatment and

---

[25] Cohen, Eliot A. & John Gooch. *Military Misfortunes* (New York, NY; Free Press, 2006) 248

schools."[26]   The desired end-state of a stable and functioning democratic Iraq was endangered during the first few years of the occupation due to the focus on enemy conditions over that of others, like the collateral conditions of the civilian population.

General David Petraeus' reinvigorated the counterinsurgency effort with greater emphasis on civil engagements between troops and Iraqi citizens, "You can't commute to this fight… Living among the people is essential to securing them and defeating the insurgents… patrol on foot and engage the population. Situational awareness can only be guaranteed by interacting with people face-to-face, not separated by ballistic glass."[27]   By providing greater emphasis to other conditions beyond just the enemy, the new counterinsurgency doctrine had made headway in garnering local support for the mission, and more importantly, the Iraqi government. This was a major condition for the desired end-state, and in retrospect, should have been the major strategic objective from the beginning.   Moreover, this shows the importance that the desired end-state has towards the COA development process, because it provides insight into what conditions are required for success.

Time

When developing COAs it is important to understand and anticipate the duration in which operations will take place.   The world transforms over time as important people and events shape their environments.   Development of plans are based on specific conditions within the operational environment that dictate the objectives, decisions points, and required effects necessary to achieve the desired end-state.   As time progresses the operational environment will change in relation to the world and the initial conditions of the environment in which plans were developed may no longer be the same.   As a result, there may be significant flaws

---

[26] Cohen, 249

[27] Bergen, Perter, "How Petraeus changed the U.S. military" *CNN*, Accessed June 23,2014. http://www.cnn.com/2012/11/10/opinion/bergen-petraeus-legacy/.

with the standing plan if it is unable to adapt to the changes in the environment. Thus during COA develop, planners must incorporate time as a variable in their planning, and anticipate how it affects the operational environment.

Time is a variable that has omnipresence throughout the operational environment; indeed the universe, and exist more as a perception than a system. Whereas desired end-states produce objectives, enemy conditions focus targeting, and environmental conditions limit methods, the analysis of time; however, does not produce products. The variable of time simply references the changes of conditions within the operational environment. Greater duration of operations leads to more changes to conditions as the environment adapts to the effects created by those operations, as well as external influences. Obviously, planners cannot increase or decrease the flow of time, but they can alter COAs to achieve the desired end-state in a shorter period or provide it flexibility to sustain itself during change. Understanding that the conditions of the operational environment are constantly changing, the time factor comes into play in two additional ways; the duration until conditions can be affected and the ability to sustain a COA.

Depending on the means to be used and the way they are employed time becomes a factor for planners who have to incorporate deployment of resources to an operational environment. If the objectives of the desired end-state call for the deployment of military forces then the time it takes to deliver those forces into a region can affect the decision making process for tailoring them. The multi-ton assets of an armored brigade combat team can only be transported great distances via ship and rail-line, and may require weeks to move its combat power into position. An infantry brigade combat team; however, and its array of light combat vehicles and equipment can be airlifted into a theater within a few days.

In 1979, some United States military planners were concerned about Iraqi provocations throughout the Middle East, and predominantly the threat they posed to Saudi Arabia. "If the United

States' warnings and occasional muscle flexing were not enough to keep the Iraqis at bay , the United States needed to act fast to send combat forces to the region. The Iraqi troops were on the doorstep of the oil-rich states in the Gulf while American forces were half a world away."[28] Even though Iraq turned its attentions towards Iran, situations like this show the importance that time has during the COA development process, because there is a significant delay between approval and execution of a particular COA. Sometimes a path needs to be taken even though the critical events that spurred the need for that path have not transpired. The deployment of combat forces to the Middle East to counter an Iraqi attack would be at a significant disadvantage if it had not been preemptively deployed there for such a contingency.

In regards to the duration of operations, time plays another critical factor. The political processes of a government continue to function during the execution of COAs, and planners and decision makers need to take into account their ability to sustain them during times of political change. Within democratic governments, where the opinions of the general population influence the political processes, a long and/or unpopular COA, even if critical to supporting national interests, may be put at risk during a change in the political environment. In America, it is not unheard of to see a policy instituted by an incumbent politician to be changed after failing to hold their seat from a candidate of the opposing party. Additionally, an incumbent may find it difficult to continue to support existing policy if there is significant resistance from within the legislative body of government – because of political turnover. Thus, execution of a COA for an extended period of time runs an increasing risk of failure, not just from the changing conditions within the operational environment, but from within the government executing that COA.

---

[28] Gordon, Trainor R. & Bernard E. Trainor GEN (USA). *The Generals' War* (New York, NY; Back Bay Books, 1995) 8

Enemy Conditions

Analysis and assessment of adversarial capabilities, motives, and desired ends plays an important role in the development of COAs within the JOPP. Conduct of this is through the Joint Intelligence Preparation of the Operational Environment (JIPOE) process conducted during the planning initiation and mission analysis phases of the JOPP. It frames the operational environment, and seeks to evaluate the enemy's capabilities, determine their strategic and operational objectives, and describe their most likely courses of action (MLCOA) and most dangerous courses of action (MDCOA). From these MLCOA/MDCOA military planners and their commanders can identify various priority intelligence requirements (PIR) and commander's critical information requirements (CCIR) which when identified help drive certain decisions points (DP) that shape the fight.[29]

Beyond the military aspects of enemy conditions, there is inherently a relationship between them and the rest of the operational environment. While local populations may or may not be supportive of the enemy, they do have an impact to the manner in which their organization functions throughout the area of operations. Providing or denying safe havens for transnational threats to pull recruits and resources, and giving legitimacy to policies of belligerent states is an aspect in which enemy and collateral conditions are in relation. Additional support or hindrance towards an enemy organization can be found through third-party and friendly organizations; state or non-state, which provides the alternatives towards new ways and means for conducting operations. By gauging the relationship between those conditions and the enemy, strengths and vulnerabilities become apparent, and aid in the targeting process.

During Desert Storm, the planners of the air campaign were able to assess the nature of the Iraqi IADS and C2 nodes. They understood what was required to deliver the desired effects on

---

[29] Wade, Norman W. *The Joint Forces Operations and Doctrine: SMARTbook 3rd Edition* (Lakeland, FL: The Lightning Press, 2012) 3-57

particular enemy systems in order to achieve their objectives. Assessing that defeating enemy IADS and neutralizing those C2 elements would open up the remainder of the country to increased air attack, they developed a COA that sought to strike all these targets in parallel. Traditional attack methodology would have focused on defeating all IADS prior to engaging C2 nodes, the coalition *Black Hole* planning group believed that through both a thorough understanding of the nature of the Iraqi defenses and the availability of friendly stealth and precision weaponry that they could create a collapse of the enemy system within a much shorter period. "The ideal application of force in a parallel attack strategy to achieve rapid dominance involves the application of force against all targets in each target system at one time," as stated by Deptula, "With correct identification of target systems and appropriate targets critical to each system, if each target is hit, the effects desired within each system will likely occur."[30] By understanding the enemy conditions, *Black Hole* was able to determine how to target them.

Third-Party Conditions

Due to the nature of globalization in the 21st Century, it is hard to argue that any particular operational environment is devoid of external influencers. Even the most isolated Amazonian tribes have representatives that work on their behalf. Both state and non-state actors can have stakes in the operational environment that drive them to become involved in some fashion. Organizations can benefit through economic support, military assistance, and diplomatic leveraging or they can hinder through sanctions, military action, and political ostracizing.

Operations Enduring Freedom and Iraqi Freedom saw increasing levels of Muslim extremists pouring into Afghanistan and Iraq in order to conduct Jihad against American and NATO/Coalition forces as well as their local national governments. Even though America and its partners going into these operational

---

[30] Deptula, 14

environments did not do so with religious intentions that did not necessarily prevent potential rivals from shaping the environment into a religious war.

Additionally, external influencers may act within an operational environment against other third-party players. DIME instruments of national power, though non-state actors can employ them, have been used by third-party entities during critical engagements between other nations. Proxy wars, or engagements through proxy, are the concept that a state or non-state organization can hinder or upset a rival through the support of their current adversary. The organization engaging their enemy through a proxy can go about it using either overt or covert methods, and the nature of that support can be military, non-military, or both. The overall goal is a weakening in the enemy's instruments of national power through a prolonged engagement within the operational environment, and prevention of them achieving their desired end-state. Beyond sharing a common enemy; however, the proxy may or may not share mutual interests with their supporting organization. Regardless, the support of the proxy adds a new dimension to the enemy's strengths by potentially providing them diplomatic clout, informational assistance, military aid, and/or economic support.

During the Korean War, as the Republic of Korea (ROK) and United Nations forces battled with the North Korean People's Army (NKPA), which had been bolstered by Soviet arms during the pre-war build up, they also had to contend with both covert support by the Soviet Union as well as overt military support by the Chinese. While the Soviets provided MiG-15s and fighter pilots to help contend with American air power over North Korea, the Chinese deployed nearly a quarter million infantrymen in November 1950 as UN Forces approached the Yalu River; separating North Korea from Manchuria. Though poorly equipped they were significant in number to sufficiently surround and defeat ROK and US regiments forcing the UN armies to withdraw south. After American support of the collapsing ROK Army resulted in the strategic defeat of the NKPA after successful amphibious landings at the South Korean port of Inchon, China's switch from concerned third-party observer to an active combatant was not a guarantee. Even as the NKPA lost a majority of its combat power in the south, and it appeared that ROK forces may attempt to unify the peninsula by crossing the 38th Parallel, and securing the north, there were conditions to which the Chinese would not get involved.

This concern was clear when, on 3 October 1950, Chou En-lai, the Chinese foreign minister, called Ambassador Sadar K. M. Panikkar of India to his office. He told him that, if the United States or United Nations forces crossed the 38th Parallel, China would send troops to defend North Korea. He said that this action would not be taken if only South Korean troops crossed the parallel... On 10 October, a week later, Peiping radio broadcast a declaration of Chinese intentions that repeated this warning. Five days later a reliable source reported that Moscow would have a surprise awaiting the American force if it approached the northern border of Korea.[31]

General Douglas McArthur, and the rest of United Nations Command, dismissed the warnings as hollow threats and decided to push on through the 38th Parallel alongside the ROK Army. In hindsight we can determine that the decision made was incorrect, because United Nations forces were not equipped to handle the nature of the new threat if it had, and did, prove to be credible. Though there had been speculation of Soviet involvement in the skies, there were overt signs of Chinese potential involvement on the ground which would have an evident impact on the course of the war.

In December 1979, the Soviet Union invaded the nation of Afghanistan with the desired end-state being to reestablish a pro-Soviet government. During a coup, then President of the Democratic Republic of Afghanistan, Nur Muhammad Taraki, was killed by his Deputy Prime Minister Hafizullah Amin in September of that year,

---

[31] Appleman, Roy E. LTC (USA). *Disaster in Korea* (College Station, TX; Texas A&M, 1989) 7-8

and took control over the country. In order to consolidate his power, Amin led a socio-political campaign in which he released thousand of personnel, previously imprisoned under Taraki, and repressed all would be dissenters to his relative dictatorship. These activities would not produce the desired effects that were intended, and Amin's administration began losing the support of the population.[32] Additionally, some members of the politburo believed that Amin's attempts to garner support from the United States for his regime was creating potential threat to the Soviet Union. The Soviets feared this association with the United States occurring on its southern border and the general destabilization of the region as a result of Amin's actions pressured the Soviets to intervene in Afghanistan. The "Soviet desire to subjugate the Afghan communist party and to remove Amin and his key supporters,"[33] as stated by David Gibbs from the University of Arizona, were the military objectives by which the Soviets would achieve their desired end-state.

Third-party support of the Mujahedeen during the Soviet occupation of Afghanistan became a significant problem for Soviet armed forces, because it was through this support that these insurgents were able to persist. The Soviets attempted to reduce the threat of enemy attack by deploying heavily armed and armored SU-25 ground attack aircraft and Mi-24 attack helicopters. They were sufficient to support Soviet ground operations, and defeat Mujahedeen attacks; however, when the United States CIA started equipping the fighters with FIM-92 Stinger man-portable air defense systems the Soviets began losing aircraft at an unsustainable rate. Though it is argued whether or not the edge these systems provided to the insurgency was the critical factor in the Soviet withdrawal from Afghanistan there was no doubt that it was a significant loss in military hardware.[34]

---

[32] Brecher, Michael & Jonathan Wilkenfeld. A Study in Crisis. (Ann Arbor, MI; University of Michigan Press, 1997) 357

[33] Gibbs, David N. "Afghanistan: The Soviet Invasion Retrospect" *International Politics* (Tucson, AZ; University of Arizona, 2000) 236

[34] Gibbs, 237

The final note to make on third-party conditions is that when planning for operations in one particular environment those actions that are undertaken can have an effect in another. For example, in preparation for what was seen as an inevitable showdown amongst the nations of Europe, at the onset of the First World War, the British reneged on a contractual deal with the Turks. The contract between the Ottomans and the British was for the purchase to two dreadnoughts which would become the flagships of the revitalized Turkish Navy. Their government couldn't afford the purchase so instead reached out to its own population for assistance. From major cities to small towns, donation campaigns were a success as their people were imbued in nationalistic spirit and a hope in a stronger Ottoman Empire, which had been on the decline since their costly conflict in the Balkans. They had raised enough money for the purchase, and that money was delivered to England, along with the Turkish crews whom would sail them back, when the British failed to deliver on the contract. "At this point – to be precise on August 3rd [1914], the eve of the outbreak of war – Winston Churchill, the First Lord of the Admiralty, announced to the Turks that he could not make delivery; in the interests of national security the two ships had been requisitioned by the British Navy."[35]

In reneging on the contract, and keeping the ships for their own navy, the British were bolstering their own capabilities in preparation for the war with the Germans and Austrians. In doing so; however, the betrayal felt by the Turkish government and its people pushed them closer to the Central Powers, and Baron Hans von Wangenheim; German ambassador to the Ottomans, used this to their advantage. A series of standoffs between the British and German navies in the Mediterranean soon lead to a contractual deal between the Germans and Turks in which the German ships, the *Goeben*, the *Breslau*, and their crews, became part of the Turkish Navy. After an incident in the Dardanelles and the Black Sea, events finally

---

[35] Moorehead, Alan. *Gallipoli* (Harper, NY; The Nautical & Aviation Publishing Company of America, 1956) 25-26

brought the Ottoman Empire into the war on the side of the Central Powers on August 30th. The Turks had no compulsion or desire to go to war; however, they felt compelled over a sense of betrayal by the British and the resulting opportunities offered to them by the Germans. In trying to strengthen their own navy the British created a cascade of effects that, after German diplomatic and military involvement, created a new enemy for the allies.[36]

Collateral Conditions

When military planners discuss collateral conditions, it is usually in regards to collateral damage considerations that occur because of military operations. In November 2010's *Field Manual 3-60: The Targeting Process* the word *collateral* is used twenty-six times, and in twenty-one of those cases it is in relation to collateral damage. The other five instances terms like *collateral effects*, *risk*, and *data* reference the impact that operations have in everything other than kinetic damage. The repetitive use of *collateral damage* belies its true nature, because the desire to negate or mitigate the unintended destructive effects on collateral personnel and infrastructure is intended to reduce unwanted non-kinetic effects; like loss of legitimacy for friendly operations or bolstering of support for enemy organizations. While referring to the targeting process, it is stated in *FM 3-60* that "adhering to [targeting principles] should increase the probability of creating desired effects while diminishing undesired or adverse collateral effects."[37]

Collateral conditions in the context of this thesis refer to not only the unintended or incidental involvement of non-military persons and infrastructure, but also primarily the relationships they hold with one another, and other variables, within the operational environment. Even when there is no creation of damage of a collateral nature, if the effects of any action is observable by collateral

---

[36] Moorehead, 29-31
[37] Department of the Army. *Field Manual 3-60: Targeting* (Washington, D.C.: Government Printing Office, 2010) 1-2

elements then you have the creation of collateral effects. For example, if American military forces engaged with and destroyed an al-Qaeda terror cell on American soil then it would have starkly different collateral effects than if the operation had occurred in the caves of Tora Bora in eastern Afghanistan. Even if the nature, conduct, and results of these operations were the same, the differences in collateral effects would be much more apparent. The free press in the United States is more robust and with the interconnectivity amongst most of the population, collateral effects can permeate throughout the entire society relatively quick, whereas, the disconnected and segregated communities of Afghanistan the effects would be much more localized. Additionally, the hardiness of these societies is inherently different, and what may be breaking news in America may just be a standard affair in Afghanistan.

Beyond the effects of collateral damage internal to the area of operations there is also an interrelated effect between collateral effects and third-party observers. States may try to reduce the negative political implications of combat by reducing unintended destruction to collateral concerns. As a result, modern states who tout about having technologically advanced military capabilities to combat foes may suffer loss of face as a result of collateral damage. This has spurned the teaching of the Law of Armed Conflict (LOAC), as directed by the Department of Defense Law of War (LOW) program. "The law of war encompasses all international law for the conduct of hostilities binding on the United States or its individual citizens, including treaties and international agreements to which the United States is a party, and applicable customary international law."[38] With the advent of precision weaponry there has been greater emphasis on the limitation of weapon usage, and their destructive effects, to military targets. In fact, since Operation Desert Storm and the creation of the EBO concept the need to limit unintended or undesired collateral effects have spurned the

---

[38] Department of Defense. *Directive 2311.01E: DoD Law of War Program.* Accessed 28 June, 2014. http://www.dtic.mil/whs/directives/corres/pdf/231101e.pdf

development of more accurate and precise targeting and weapon systems.

During Operation Allied Force, NATO's intelligence of the operational environment suffered from out-of-date maps and low-resolution aerial photography which made it difficult to discern military and non-military assets. In one incident, NATO air forces inadvertently struck the Chinese embassy in Belgrade, utilizing a GPS-guided bomb, instead of a legitimate Yugoslavian military target. Regardless of mistakes, Serb forces were so embedded within the urban area that, without precise targeting data and weapons, it would be nigh impossible to avoid adverse collateral effects, but NATO and the United States were still bound by LOW to do their utmost to mitigate loss of civilian lives and infrastructure. Problems of collateral damage were compounded by Serbian military's counter-air technique of *hugging* collateral concerns, in that those enemy forces used proximity to civilian structures and populations to dissuade attacks upon their assets.[39]

Environmental Conditions

Analysis of environmental conditions occurs during the second step of the JIPOE as planners describe the factors that make up the operational environment, and those environmental factors include both natural and manufactured elements.[40] These conditions affect both military and non-military operations in various ways, but mainly through the support or hindrance of the means available to conduct those operations. Higher elevations affect the altitude ceiling of many aircraft, and lesser powered helicopters and planes may be forced to operate at lower altitudes. Roads, rivers, mountains, and buildings can determine the path in which ground forces maneuver. Water tables, soil quality, and weather can limit or promote certain types of crops for agriculture, and availability of natural resources can

---

[39] Cordesman, Anthony H. *The Lessons and Non-Lessons of the Air and Missile Campaign in Kosovo* (Westport, CT; Praeger Publishing, 2001) 356
[40] Wade, 3-56

dictate the nature of trade, industry, and commerce.

The environment thus plays an important role in the conduct of any human action. When planners are trying to determine the necessary COAs to create a desired end-state there must be an understanding of these environmental conditions, and how they impact what effects need to be created and which assets can create those effects. If the desired end-state requires that communities within the operational environment convert agriculture from production of illicit to staple crops then certain information will be required. What is the pH and nutrition level of the soil? What is the annual rainfall for that region? Do their farming communities have the capability to plant, grow, and harvest certain crops? Is there a greater incentive to grow staple foodstuffs instead of illegal products? If any of these questions are unanswered then success of that particular element of a COA is at risk.

For military operations, the environmental conditions can shape how certain assets are utilized and alter the effects they create. On the 19th of August 1942 during the ill-fated raid on the French coastal city of Dieppe, British and Canadian forces suffered a significant defeat due to lack of intelligence and a limited understanding what amphibious operations required. The primary mission of this raid was not simply to create a foothold, but to test new concept and technologies developed by the allies prior to a greater amphibious operation that would happen at a latter, yet to be determined date. The severity of the defeat; however, taught them a very important lesson. For environmental conditions, the consistency of the pebbly beaches, and height of the shingles on the approach to the city, meant that many of the tanks of the 14th Calgary Armored Regiment became bogged down on the beachhead, and were unable to provide direct fire support for the infantry moving inland. As the only significant form of firepower available, the infantry were not able to make progress securing the area and were forced to withdrawal after facing strong German resistance.[41]

---

[41] Juno Beach Centre. *The Dieppe Raid.* Accessed June 29, 2014.

Military forces may be limited by the conditions of the environment; however, they may also have to means to alter those conditions. During Operation Allied Force, when it appeared that Yugoslavian President Slobodan Milosevic would not come to NATO's terms after continual aerial attack upon his ground forces, and successes of the Kosovo Liberation Army (KLA), allied military leadership began planning for a ground option should it be necessary. In order to defeat the enemy's armored forces and safeguard its own soldiers, NATO would have to utilize heavy armored units for the attack. The route through Albania's Kukes Mountains, however, did not have the durability to support to the weight of the forces NATO would be bringing, and might collapse under the stress. "US, German, and Italian military engineers cooperated in a contingency effort to strengthen the road through Kukes to take armored traffic... This effort was essential because the road could not support M1A1 tank traffic without such improvement."[42] While ground forces were not necessary to bring Milosevic to terms the ability of heavily armored NATO forces entering into the fight may have produced the desired effect; a desired effect that would not have been possible without accounting for the environmental impact upon military operations. But as always, the environmental conditions do not only affect military means. They also impact the employment of non-military means as well.

The Provincial Reconstruction Teams (PRT) in Afghanistan for years has tried to eradicate the illicit drug trade emanating from the country. Other than the commercial benefits of growing poppy plants for the production of opium the environmental conditions also make more licit forms of crop production (e.g. fruits, vegetables, and grains) difficult. In the case of Afghanistan, the illicit drug production as a result of collateral conditions; primarily commercial and agricultural, and environmental conditions; primarily rainfall and soil richness, led to its continued persistence even as the United

---

http://www.junobeach.org/canada-in-wwii/articles/the-dieppe-raid/
[42] Cordesman, 244

States and the Afghan government made attempts to eradicate opium crops and convert them towards food and textile production. As the United States has begun its draw down of military forces, and economic aid to Afghanistan there has been a steady increase in opium production as a result, because without a change to those initial conditions, or presence of third-party support against them, the operational environment has naturally began shifting back towards those conditions.[43]

Naturally, illicit drug trade in Afghanistan also affected the Taliban. Having near complete control of the trade of opium within the area, including contact with merchants who could export the product out of the region, the Taliban benefitted by the drug trade in that the economic support it provided had paid for large quantities of military hardware and helped bribe corrupt government officials. Thusly, environmental conditions not only had a direct impact on their military operations, (e.g. movement of fighters), but also had STO effects upon its economy. When rainfall was plentiful in opium producing regions then the direct effect was an increase in crop yield[44], while STO effects were greater volume of trade and an increase in funds to the Taliban. Conversely, when rainfall was limited the resulted cascade of effects meant that the Taliban's yearly income from the drug trade diminished.

From the natural boundaries of the Hellespont canalizing Persian forces into the Greek phalanxes at Thermopylae to the man-made trenches of the First World War providing cover for troops against the new and destructive weapons of industrialization, environmental conditions that military planners need to both anticipate and exploit where possible. The bounties provided to Egyptian Kingdoms by the Nile River to the economic downturn of Southern and Midwest America, as a result of the Dust Bowl, had

---

[43] Afghanistan Ministry of Counter Narcotics & United Nations Office on Drugs and Crime. *Afghanistan Opium Survey 2013,* 18

[44] Afghanistan Ministry of Counter Narcotics & United Nations Office on Drugs and Crime, Accessed 04 July, 2014. http://www.unodc.org/documents/crop-monitoring/Afghanistan/Afghan_report_Summary_Findings_2013.pdf. 14

direct non-military effects upon their societies which further resulted in STO effects upon all sectors. Regardless, of advancement in technology or understanding of the natural world, environmental conditions continue to affect the nature of military and non-military means, and thus greatly impact the way we achieve the desired end-state.

Friendly Conditions

After understanding the nature of the operational environment through analysis and assessment of the other variables the final element are the ways and means available to friendly forces. Based on time, enemy, third-party, collateral, and environmental conditions, friendly capabilities will need to be utilized in such a fashion as to create a change in those conditions necessary to bring about the desired end-state. The key to the proper application of capabilities comes from the understanding of the relationships of those other variables in order to create the desired effects within the operational environment. Applying military force against an enemy target can produce a desired effect; however, it may also produce adverse or collateral effects upon local populations whose support is required for the desired end-state. Understanding those relationships, and the effects necessary to shape them towards our ends, will thus assist COA development.

As with any EBA method, it is important to avoid acknowledging capabilities prior to determining desired effects in order to avoid a system bias. For the development of the air campaign for Operation Desert Storm, Deptula stated that, "country of origin, service component, special operations force, missile, aircraft, or helicopter – did not matter – desired effect and system capability were the drivers of weapon selection for the air campaign – true jointness in action."[45] Proper application of EBA focuses on the effects required to achieve ends, not the means available to bring about ends, because the focusing on the availability of means creates the potential to drive

---

[45] Deptula, 24

COA development instead of the requisite effects.

A major issue with the conduct of Operation Allied Force, the air campaign against the Yugoslav military in Kosovo, was that internal political pressure forced NATO leaders to choose a strictly air and missile campaign from the beginning instead of opening up the possibility of ground forces. Even as the campaign was failing to bring Milosevic to the diplomatic terms, SECDEF William Cohen cautioned the Supreme Allied Commander, Europe (SACEUR) US Army General Wesley Clark, prior to an Allied summit to discuss, "Nothing about ground forces. We have to make this air campaign work, or we'll both be writing our resumes."[46] The reason given for the slow progress made by the air campaign, as mentioned previously in the section on collateral conditions, was that Yugoslavian military forces were embedded within the Kosovar population making it difficult for NATO air forces to attack them without accepting risk of collateral effects. Air strikes were reducing in number not just because of fewer targets available, but of restriction emplaced on them to reduce collateral damage; especially after the Chinese embassy incident. For the months leading up to Milosevic finally accepting terms on the 10th of June 1999, Clark gave final credit to its success not just because of the persistence of the air and missile campaign, but to additional factors as well, one of which was the increasing threat of ground intervention which would have finally destroyed the remainder of Milosevic's forces within Kosovo.[47]

Additionally, when working in conjunction with allies or partners they may have their own considerations for the desired end-state or application of elements of national power. For example, as America entered into the Second World War it had already been determined that they would engage in a *Europe-First* grand strategy, and attempt to defeat the Germans and Italians before putting forth full effort against the Japanese. United States President Franklin Roosevelt and

---

[46] Clark, Wesley K. GEN (USA). *Waging Modern War* (New York, NY; PublicAffairs, 2001) 269
[47] Clark, 405-406

British Prime Minister Winston Churchill understood that American and British military effort would have to be unified in order to combat the well-equipped and experienced enemy. In late 1942, there was; however, conflict between the respective military planners on how best to defeat the Germans. The Americans guided by the thinking of popular and well-intended military leaders, like General George C. Marshall, believed a direct attack into Nazi-held Europe was the most prudent decision. In his thinking, "[Marshall] viewed the strategic problem in simple terms: the United States should concentrate its military might on achieving a successful lodgment on the European continent as soon as possible."[48] Americans were not too fond of the prospect of a long drawn-out conflict, and would have preferred to have thrown its full effort into a single decisive operation to end it quickly. Conversely, British military leaders like Field Marshall Alan Brooke, understood the complexities of attempting to conduct such operations into mainland Europe, via their lessons from the failed raid at Dieppe, and the idea that in order to support such an operation would require significant British military power which they wouldn't dare risk at what they thought was such an ill-timed endeavor.[49]

The British preferred to skirt around the German and Italian periphery, via North Africa, and move up through Italy. They believed that such a maneuver would significantly weaken the Germans by fighting them on more equal footing, and eventually free up the sea-routes for British supply lines to reach out to the wealth of their remaining empire. When it looked as if Marshall was going to alter the grand strategy and shift focus away from Germany to Japan, "[Roosevelt] intervened and overruled his military advisers. Roosevelt gave his generals a direct order to support the British proposal for landings along the coast of French North Africa. The President's reasoning was largely based on political necessity."[50] The

---

[48] Murray, Williamson. "Triumph of Operation Torch" *World War II Magazine* (Leesburg, VI; Weider History Group 2002) 44

[49] Murray, 45

[50] Murray, 45

friendly conditions of the European Theater, and the President's understanding that success within that operational environment hinged on British cooperation, he acquiesced to the desired ways of a friendly nation in order to support America's own desired end-state; the defeat of Nazi German and a quick end to conflict.

IV
THE OPERATIONAL ENVIRONMENT
AND THE JIPOE

From the aforementioned conditions we can see how the attributes of the operational environment can greatly impact the nature of effects created, and through them the ability to achieve the desired end-state. The conditions that are present and the relationships they hold within that environment become the structure by which actions cascade, and until this structure is understood then planners will not be able to fully understand what effects will be created. Conditions and their relationships are understood in three different ways: conditions are known and relationship determined, conditions are known and relationships are undetermined, and conditions are unknown and relationships undetermined.

The JOPP is unable to determine the nuances of the operational environment due to preferential knowledge towards the conditions directly related towards military means. The JIPOE provides the commander information in regards to enemy centers of gravity (COG), and how they relate to the operational environment. Beyond enemy conditions, however, not much consideration is given towards collateral, third-party, and environmental conditions. When they do, it is in relation to enemy conditions. As stated in *Joint Publication 2-01-3: Joint Intelligence Preparation of the Operational Environment*, "The primary purpose of JIPOE is to support joint operation planning, execution, and assessment by identifying, analyzing, and assessing the adversary's COGs, critical vulnerabilities, capabilities, decisive points, limitations, intentions, COAs, and reactions to friendly operations based on a holistic view of the operational environment."[51] Developing the JIPOE allows planners to develop products necessary to the development of COAs, and facilitates it creation by determining nine attributes of an enemy's potential COAs, capabilities, and desired ends.

1. *The idiosyncrasies and decision-making patterns of the adversary strategic leadership and field commanders.*
2. *The adversary's strategy, intentions, or strategic concept of operations, which should include the adversary's desired end state, perception of friendly vulnerabilities, and adversary intentions regarding those vulnerabilities.*
3. *The composition, dispositions, movements, strengths, doctrine, tactics, training, and combat effectiveness of major adversary forces that can influence friendly actions in the theater and operations areas.*
4. *The adversary's principal strategic and operational objectives and lines of operation.*
5. *The adversary's strategic and operational sustainment capabilities.*
6. *COGs and decision points throughout the adversary's operational and strategic depths.*
7. *The adversary's ability to conduct IO and use or access data from all systems.*
8. *The adversary's regional strategic vulnerabilities.*
9. *The adversary's capability to conduct asymmetric attacks against friendly global critical support nodes (e.g., electric power grids, oil and gas pipelines, pre-positioned supply depots).*[52]

While the aforementioned products of the JIPOE help develop an understanding of both enemy conditions, and the relationships between the enemy and the operational environment, that is the

---

[51] JP 2-01.3, III-1
[52] JP 2-01.3, III-2-3

extent to which it supports COA development. The current JOPP fails because the processes that feed it information necessary to plan (e.g., JIPOE) attempt to operationalize the process by segregating the impact on conditions of a military nature and those of a non-military nature. For example, in the six-phase model for joint operations there are clear delineations between the intent for each phase. The third phase, known as domination or combat operations phase, "focuses on breaking the enemy's will for organized resistance or, in noncombat situations, control of the operational environment."[53] This is followed by the fourth phase, or stability phase, which, "is required when there is no fully functional, legitimate civil governing authority present. The joint force may be required to perform limited local governance, integrating the effort of other supporting/ contributing multinational, IGO, NGO, or [United States Government] department and agency participants until legitimate local entities are functioning."[54]

One can easily discern the differences in objectives within the third and fourth phases of military operations; however, this doesn't necessarily mean that the actions that occur in the third phase do not have cascading effects that affect fourth phase operations. From the beginning of phase zero, shaping operations, to the complete of phase five, enabling civil authority, conditions of the operational environment are continuously changing based on the direct and STO effects created by preceding military action and the relationships of the other conditions. When the JIPOE helped developed the COA during the JOPP they created a COA that was focused on military matters, instead of a holistic analysis of the operational environment in which all the conditions are interrelated. This means that while planning strategic guidance for third phase operations, actions and their effects are planned primarily in relation to those enemy conditions that were assessed through JIPOE. It neglects the

---

[53] Joint Staff, *Joint Publication 5: Joint Operations Planning* (Washington, D.C.; Government Printing Office, 2011, xxiv
[54] JP 5-0, xxiv

importance that other, non-military, conditions of the operational environment play towards achieving the desired end-state. What results is that there is less effort to determine the correlation to the actions taken in phase three on non-military conditions (e.g., collateral, third-party, environmental) and how those effects translate into the changed conditions of phase four. In other words, the phased nature of operations has placed a greater emphasis on producing effects geared towards affecting enemy conditions, during the combat phase, at the expense of non-enemy conditions in later phases. This in turn threatens achievement of the desired end-state, because it fails to properly shape all conditions towards that end.

While the intent of the military arm of national power to focus strictly on military related actions and effects, there is an irrevocable connection between the effects they produce and the systems in which it affects. The conditions and their relationships within the operational environment are interrelated regardless of attempts to separate military and non-military actions. Military actions taken against enemy targets not only generate the immediate direct effect and subsequent STO effects against those targets, but additional STO effects are generated against other non-military conditions. Similarly, non-military actions against non-military targets not only generate their own direct and STO effects upon those systems, but planners may be able to discern an actual STO effect generated against enemy systems as a result. The operational environment is a complex system-of-systems in which there are more conditions at play than just that of friends and foes. If the JIPOE is unable to provide the necessary information required to develop COAs that take into account all conditions within the operational environment then the JOPP will not reliably determine how to shape the conditions needed to achieve the desired end-state. A question is then raised, how can we adapt to JOPP to account for all conditions and assist in the development of COAs that achieve the desired end-state?

V

THE EFFECTS-BASED BOARD

Every condition affects the operational environment in such nuanced ways that in order to determine the nature of those conditions, and their relationships, we need to establish a planning group that develops and assesses a holistic understanding of that environment. The COCOM is the level of command to which deliberate and crisis action plans are developed, and from whom strategic guidance is passed down to subordinate organizations which affect the ability of subordinates to shape the conditions required for the desired end-state. A planning group with that holistic understanding of the operational environment would best be utilized at that COCOM level to assist, assess, and provide advice to planners and commanders during the COA development phase of those campaign plans. It will allow planners to match calculated means, either military or non-military, to achieve desired effects based on all conditions of the operational environment; not just enemy conditions. In this way the plans produced by joint force staff and approved by the Combatant Commander (CCDR) provide the most effective COAs to achieve the desired end-state.

Since the group provides a forum to which planners can receive guidance in order to coordinate sets of action in order to shape the conditions of the operational environment the group's intent is inherently related to the concept of the EBA. Due to this emphasis on calculated actions and desired effects, from hence forth this group will be referred to as the Effects-Based Board (EBB). The purpose of the EBB will be to provide a necessary forum to which planners can vet their concepts of the operation, receive guidance on particular systems within the operational environment, and overall, provide guidance to staffers and the commander as to the viability of certain COAs to shaped conditions required to achieve the desired end-state.

The sole purpose of the EBB is to provide guidance to the COCOM for the purpose of COA development, and potentially further guidance during the development of fragmentary orders (FRAGO). They are not to assume the duties of the joint staff in the drafting of COAs, and they are not the approving authority for said COAs. Much akin the relationship that the Chairman of the Joint Chiefs of Staff (CJCS) has with the SECDEF and the CCDRs, the EBB is not within the command structure of the joint force and thus the chain of command from SECDEF, CCDRs, and subordinate elements remains unfettered while the EBB is present. Just like the CJCS; however, the EBB provides crucial guidance at the strategic level that can prove critical to the achievement of the overall mission. Understanding its relationship within the COCOM, as an advisory board, we still need to determine how the construct of the EBB produces a holistic understanding of the operational environment.

Looking back at the six-phase model for joint operations the final phase, enabling civil authorities, "is predominantly characterized by joint force support to legitimate civil governance in theater. The goal is for the joint force to enable the viability of the civil authority and its provision of essential services to the largest number of people in the region."[55] In others words, the desired military end-state of joint force operations is to set the conditions so that local governments within the operational environment can take over the responsibility of governance for their respective sovereign territories. By this phase the conditions should have been shaped in order to allow for a functioning, legitimate government to operate, and have

---

[55] JP 5-0, xxiv

created an environment to which its citizens can carry on with everyday activities. If the end product we are trying to create is a stable nation, or region, then it would behoove us to establish the EBB with personnel that understand what conditions and relationships are necessary to achieve that. Before this was predominately done by military service members, and a handful of interagency personnel, but the criticality of complexity of conditions and relationships within the operational environment require an equivalent class of personnel whom can handle it. Therefore, who better to make up the roster of the EBB than representation from the very departments and organizations that allow the United States to function as a legitimate nation, and global superpower?

In order to have the best understanding of the nature of conditions and relationships within the operational environment there are three requirements that the EBB needs to have. Firstly, membership within the EBB should encompass full breadth of the United States government. Liaisons from the Department of Health and Human Services providing guidance on how certain military actions may or may not affect public health services within the region can be as critical to achieving the desired end-state, as much as, military planners developing guidance on the martial effects of those same actions. Department of Homeland Security liaisons providing guidance on how to structure local government police forces can be more effective towards setting the conditions necessary for phase five, enabling civil authorities, than utilizing United States military police to handle to same duties in their stead. The large bureaucratic nature of the United States government is complex, because the vastness of conditions and relationships necessary to keep it functioning are themselves complex. As a result, the EBB needs to be a similar microcosm in which the knowledge of each department and organization that allows America to function can be applied to help develop COCOM COAs, as they themselves attempt to help establish functioning local and national governments in their respective areas of responsibility.

The second requirement is longevity of personnel. The conditions of each operational environment are unique for their regions, and they can only be properly understood through both initial and continuous analysis. A liaison from the Department of Agriculture needs both the time it takes to gain the intimate knowledge of collateral and environmental conditions that affect the agricultural sector of their operational environment, as well as, the personnel drive to immerse themselves into those studies. Members from the Department of Education need the time it takes to assess how public and private education functions both locally and regionally, and how that impacts the future of these communities. Finally, longevity of board members is important, because it allows for members from different sectors to understand how their particular area of knowledge relates to those of other areas; i.e. the relationships between conditions. While military members on the EBB may at most experience a full length tour of three years, based on career development, for their civilian counterparts it would be best to maintain membership for a longer duration. The Senior Executive Service (SES) may provide the necessary longevity key to developing a holistic understanding of the operational environment, due to their ability to occupy a seat for such durations.

The third requirement is that each department should be represented by two liaisons. The consensus the pair develops helps produce better advice necessary for COA development. Additionally, should one of the two be unable to sit in on the EBB during COA development, either from illness or leave, then the EBB at the very least can receive guidance from the remainder. Understanding that all these requirements will lead to an effective board to which the COCOM can both receive guidance, and vet COAs against, the final step is to determine all the departments and organizations that will be represented.

The Membership of the EBB

The makeup of this organization will encompass a vast array of members from different departments, organizations, and foreign countries. As a result, a layout of the membership of the EBB will be broken down into six categories: Geographical and Functional COCOMs, Department of Defense, Department of State, National Intelligence Agencies, Other Organizations, and Foreign Elements. Next to each shows the number of members from that area that would be within the EBB; basically number of organizations multiplied by two liaisons.

Geographical and Function COCOMs [18 personnel]
- United States Northern Command (USNORTHCOM)
- United States Southern Command (USSOUTHCOM)
- United States European Command (USEUCOM)
- United States Africa Command (USAFRICOM)
- United States Central Command (USCENTCOM)
- United States Pacific Command (USPACOM)
- United States Special Operations Command (USSOCOM)
- United States Strategic Command (USSTRATCOM)
- United States Cyber Command (USCYBERCOM)
- United States Transportation Command (USTRANSCOM)

When attached to a particular geographic COCOM, these liaisons from the other geographic and functional COCOMs provide two separate functions. First, globalization in our time means that rarely are the concerns within the area of responsibility to one organization completely segregated from that of others. International politics and transnational organizations often mean that these various COCOMs will need to share information and capabilities to tackle a common issue. Because the nation of Pakistan lies within the area of responsibility for USCENTCOM, while the nation of India lies within the area of responsibility of USPACOM, it would be natural that these two COCOMs would liaise when issues arose between these nations.

The second function is during the request for additional assets or capabilities that may be necessary to execution of a particular action within a COA. Every COCOM is unique in its structure and makeup, and may need to request the support of other COCOMs to fulfill a critical shortage or vulnerability. These liaisons, acting as representatives of their originating organizations, can communicate the needs of their attached COCOM and determine the viability of sharing assets or capabilities. Through cooperation the military planners have the potential to increase the availability and variety of means necessary to undertake certain actions during the execution of COAs.

Department of Defense (DOD) [28 personnel]
- Office of the SECDEF (OSD)
- Joint Chiefs of Staff (JCS)
- Department of the Army (DA)
- Department of the Navy (DON)
- United States Marine Corps (USMC)
- Department of the Air Force (DAF)
- United States Coast Guard (USCG)
- National Guard Bureau (NGB)
- Defense Information Systems Agency (DISA)
- Defense Logistics Agency (DLA)
- Defense Security Cooperation Agency (DSCA)
- Defense Security Service (DSS)
- Defense Threat Reduction Agency (DTRA)
- Missile Defense Agency (MDA)

Beyond the COCOM the remainder of the Department of Defense has a key role in the doctrine, organization, training, materiel, leadership and education, personnel, and facilities (DOTMLPF) necessary for the nation to defend itself from all threats. Liaisons from these organizations and agencies can provide guidance to the COCOM as to how best to establish similar organizations for legitimate civil governments within the COCOM's area of responsibility. This is of vital importance as stability and security to local communities and regions will permit other non-military capabilities to function.

Department of State (DOS) [28 personnel]
- Office of the Secretary of State (OSS)
- Department of Agriculture (DOA)
- Department of Commerce (DOC)
- Department of Education (DOED)
- Department of Energy (DOE)
- Department of Health and Human Services (DHHS)
- Department of Homeland Security (DHS)
- Department of Housing and Urban Development (HUD)
- Department of the Interior (DOI)
- Department of Justice (DOJ)
- Department of Labor (DOL)
- Department of Transportation (DOT)
- Department of the Treasury
- Department of Veteran Affairs (VA)

When building governments and the apparatuses that are necessary for them to operate, whom better than representatives of the DOS to provide the needed guidance in the establishment of a fully functioning government. When the joint force needs to help promote local agriculture and shape the training and equipping of provincial police forces the DOS has within it departments who have similar missions for our own nation.

With that experience in these particular sectors comes with it the knowledge of relationships as well. Military planners can speculate on how public education affects the workforce within a small rural community, and in turn how that workforce develops the economy and trade, but representatives from the Departments of Education, Labor, and Commerce may have a better understanding of how it all correlates. If the desired end-state is a legitimate, fully-functioning government then these members will be vital.

<u>National Intelligence Agencies</u> [12 personnel]
- Defense Intelligence Agency (DIA)
- National Security Agency (NSA)
- National Geospatial Intelligence Agency (NGIA)
- National Reconnaissance Office (NRO)
- Central Intelligence Agency (CIA)
- Federal Bureau of Investigations (FBI)

These organizations are best suited for gathering workable and actionable information necessary for other organizations to do their work. They provide the COCOM and regional government's intelligence about enemy conditions, and provide suggestions on how to impact their operations. Additionally, they can provide information on weather patterns, soil analysis, and other environmental trends that affect other sectors like agriculture, energy, and transportation. They can assess the nature of community relations between citizens, local authorities, religious leaders, and external influencers. They can determine how the effects of certain military and non-military actions will impact the conditions of the operational environment. Finally, they can support the development of intelligence gathering communities within the area of operations so that these governments can continue developing information without the constant support of the national intelligence agencies of the United States.

<u>Other Organizations</u> [mission dependent]
- US Agency for International Development (USAID)
- World Bank Group
- American Red Cross
- North Atlantic Treaty Organization (NATO)
- United Nations (UN)
- Inter and Non-Governmental Organizations (IGO/NGO)

This category includes various international, intergovernmental, and non-governmental organizations to which we can leverage support for execution of COAs. Many of these organizations have international and regional goals that are in line with our desired end-state. Leveraging these organizations, either through guidance or requests for support, can become a force multiplier, or produce effects that shape the environment to our advantage. Their contribution may be small, like the World Bank providing loans to farmers to assist in developing agriculture, to efforts much larger, like United Nations deployment of peacekeepers. This list doesn't attempt to identify all potential organizations that can support the development of COAs for the COCOM, but instead their staff will have to determine which organizations would be best included on the EBB. The nature of secrecy surrounding the development of COAs for these particular deliberate and crisis action planning will determine who can or can't be included on the EBB, but if permitted the more support and guidance the COCOM can receive from these organizations the more means it will have available to support COAs.

<u>Foreign Elements</u> [mission dependent]
- Allies
- Partners
- Host Nations
- Neutral Parties

The costs of operations can be excessive to the point of debilitating for even a nation like the United States to cover on its own. We will need to continue, as we have for more than a decade, to garner the support of our long standing allies and regional partners to shoulder the burdens of shaping the conditions of operational environments. Though we may have common interest our desired end-states may not be entirely the same, and through open discussion with their representatives we may be able to find a middle ground to which to come to an agreement. The benefit of this cooperation will be the increased availability of means to which to achieve effects for a particular COA, and in the case of regional partners, the added influence that personnel familiar with the region will help in better understanding the conditions of the operational environment. Additionally, if the mission allows it, inclusion of host nation liaisons will prove invaluable to understanding the effects of actions, and provide alternatives that their intimate knowledge of their homeland offers them.

A board of these members (Figure 1), with their diverse backgrounds and time to become acquainted with the operational environment, will provide the staff of the COCOM, and the CCDR, the necessary information required to coordinate sets of actions to shape conditions necessary for the desired end-state. The board may be quite large, consisting of more than seventy personnel, but their ability to assist in the development COAs at the beginning of deliberate and crisis action planning for the JOPP will set the COCOM, and the United States, up for success.

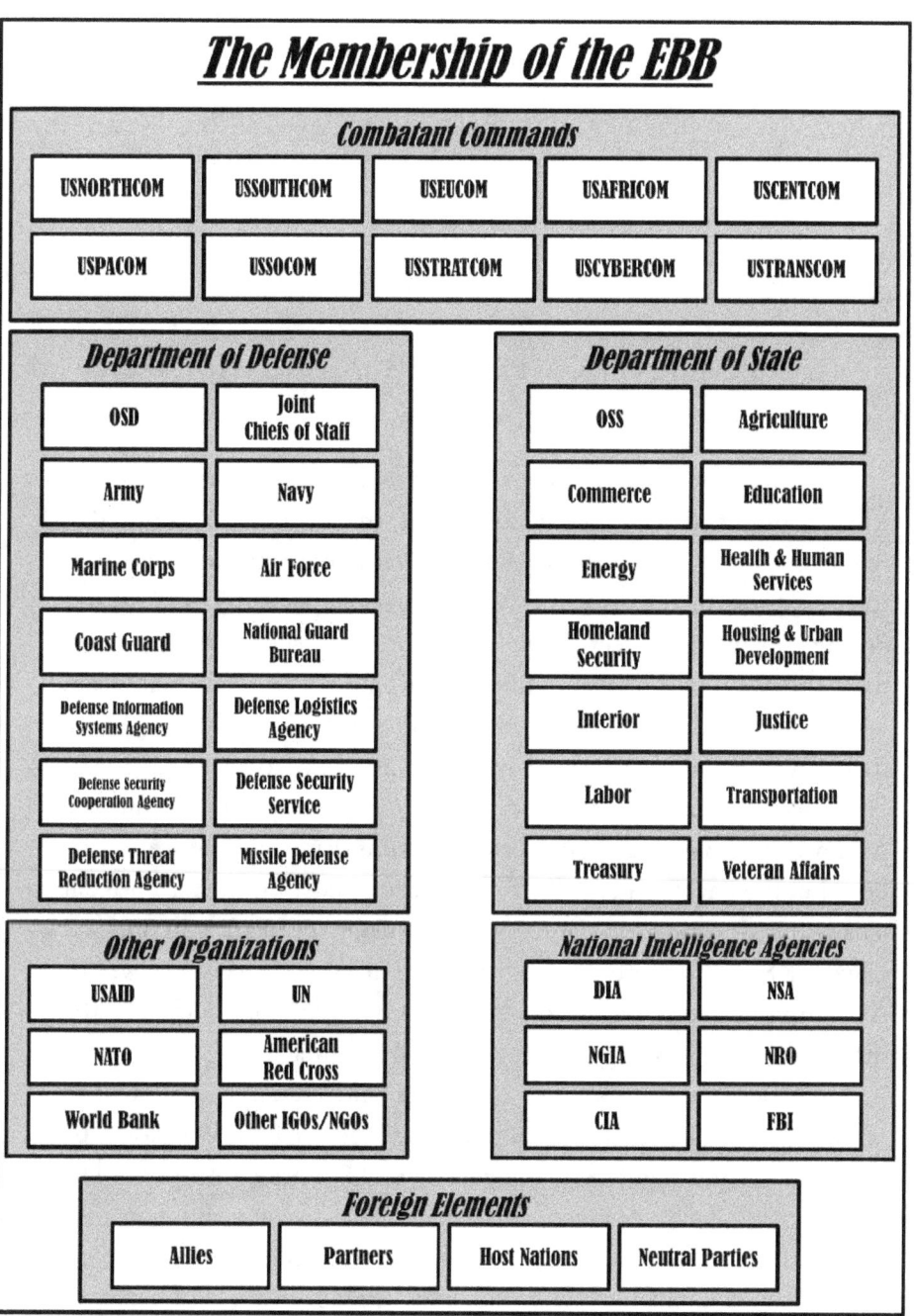

FIGURE 1

VI
INCORPORATING THE EBB INTO THE JOPP

It is logical to propose that by establishing a board of members, whose combined expertise encompasses the breadth of knowledge required to run a fully functioning government and are regionally focused, that military COAs vetted through such a board would produce plans that direct the usage of means in such a way as to set the conditions necessary for the desired end-state. That being said where would such a body reside within the COCOM? The more than seventy individual representatives assigned to the COCOM's EBB would need to be accounted for somewhere within the organization, and due to the exceptional and integral nature of the board in the development of COAs it seems most practical to place it under the direction of the COCOM's Chief of Staff and Deputy Chief of Staff (Figure 2). This situation allows a certain level of separation between the heads of the COCOM's joint staff and the members of the EBB which provides two advantages.

First, being accountable to the Chief and Deputy Chief we can reduce the likelihood of any undue influence on EBB decisions, by members of the joint staff, outside of COA working groups. The EBB's representatives need to provide assessments and guidance based their own knowledge of the operational environment's conditions and linkages, not the joint staff's COAs, in order to effectively understand the nature of that operational environment.

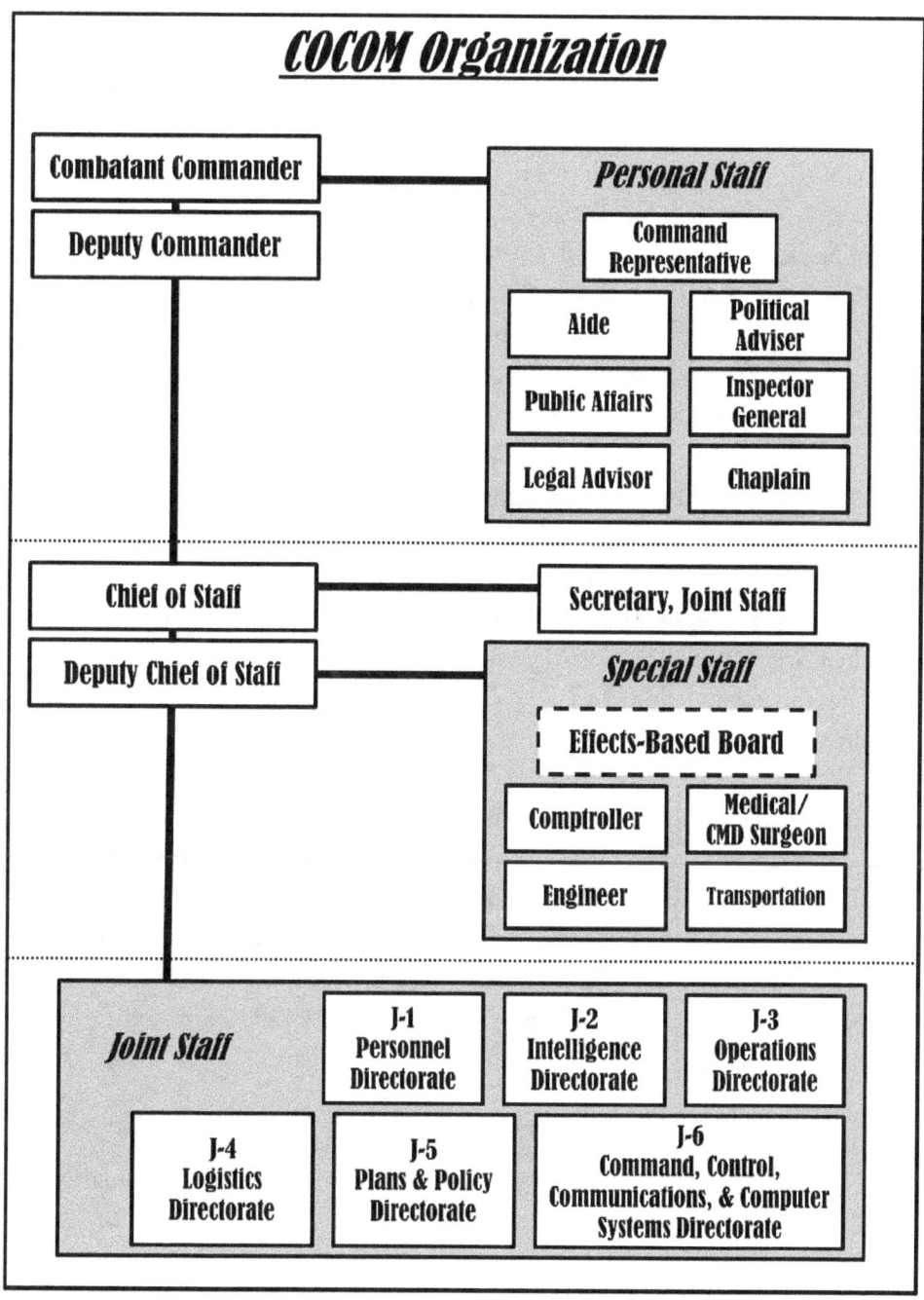

FIGURE 2

Interference by the joint staff into the EBB's initial assessments may inadvertently skew their findings, and produce ineffective evaluations of future COAs based on potential biases.

Second, falling organically underneath the special staff of the Chief and Deputy Chief of Staff gives it a greater level of importance within the organization than other working groups and decision boards within the joint force. It emphasizes the importance that military operations should always be focused towards achieving the desired end-state, which is inherently a non- military end-state. Looking back at the six-phase model for joint operations we see that after the third phase, *Dominate*, we have the fourth phase, *Stabilize*, which sees military forces begin "integrating the effort of other supporting/ contributing multinational, IGO, NGO, or USG Department and agency participants,"[56] until the final phase, *Enable Civil Authorities*, which requires predominantly non-military ways and means in order to shape the conditions for the desired end-state. Being above the joint staff, organizationally speaking, means that their assessments can hold greater weight during COA development, and can ensure that they have greatest potential to achieving those desired ends when presented to the commander.

Finally, in order to fully incorporate the EBB we need to lay out how they contribute to the JOPP, and what their duties are towards supporting the joint force in developing COAs. To do this we will follow the seven step process of the JOPP, with the EBB included, and define the due-outs and actions that are required at each step. An associated flow chart (Figure 3)[57] has been created in order to provide a visual representation of how the CCDR, joint staff, and EBB support the JOPP.

Step One: Planning Initiation

This step begins with the COCOM, either by receiving guidance from the President, SECDEF, or CJCS, or on CCDR's own accord,

---

[56] JP 5-0, xxiv
[57] JP 5-0, IV-3

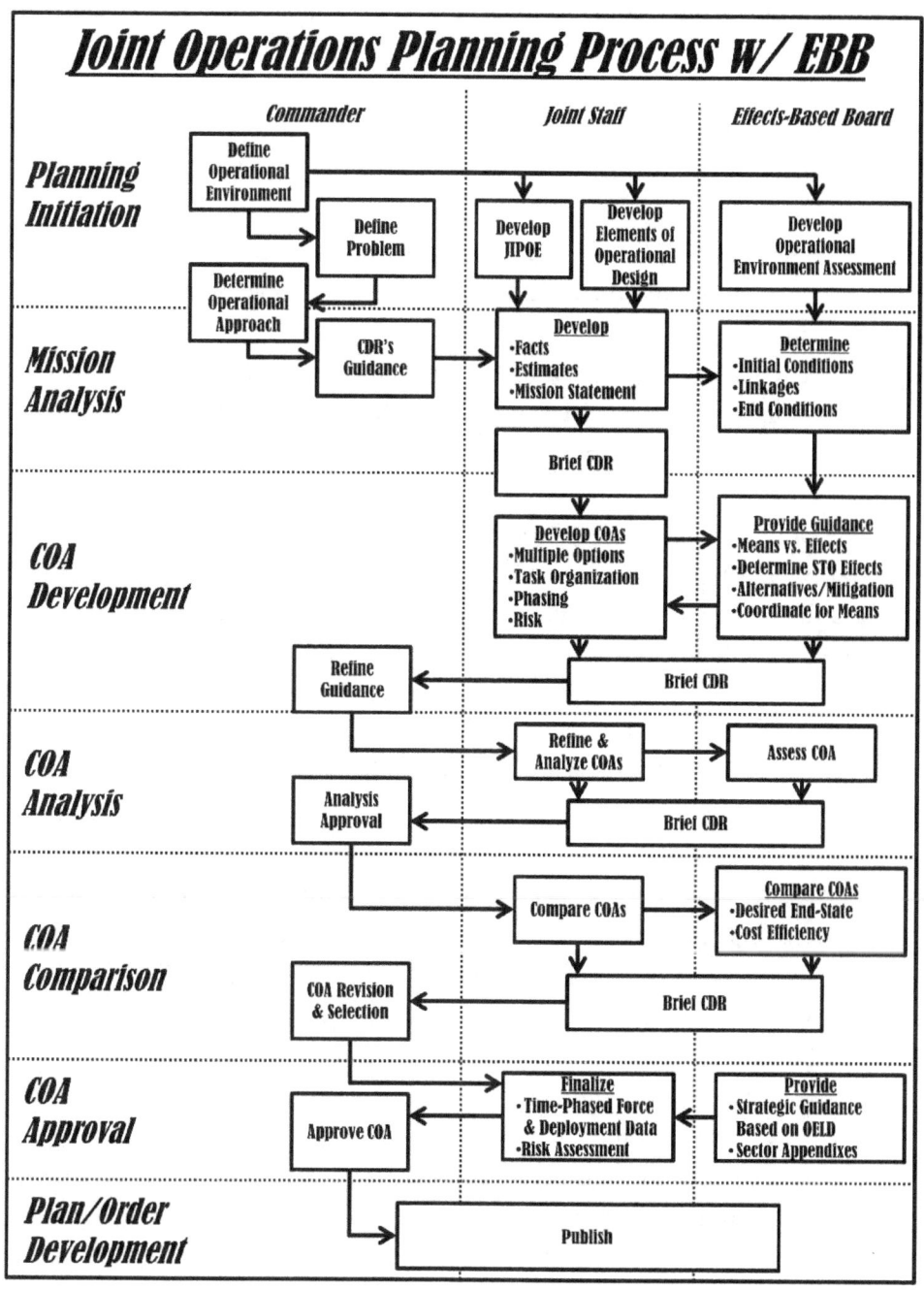

FIGURE 3

developing military options as a result of an incident or impending event.[58] The commander first defines the extent of the operational environment by bounding their area of responsibility, determining its area of influence, and area of operations. Once the operational environment has been defined to the joint staff and EBB they can begin developing their assessments. While the joint staff's intelligence and planning cells are developing the JIPOE and the elements of operational design, the EBB is developing its own assessment.

The *Operational Environment Assessment* (OEA) is developed by the EBB during the first step of the JOPP, and provides the initial products by which all proceeding steps will reference. Each pair of representatives begin to establish informational products that are relevant to their particular sector. These products, however, should not be developed from scratch as the products they use for the OEA are developed and continuously updated during standard peacetime operations. That being said, the areas of responsibility for COCOMs are vast, and the products they develop should, therefore, be numerous. By defining the extent of the operational environment, however, the CCDR has given the EBB members the limits they need to gather and finalize products relevant to this one particular mission.

Geographic and Functional COCOMs: During OEA they are gathering organizational information on their respective COCOMs, establishing a list of their capabilities, and determining if known state and transnational threats and organizations, present in their areas of responsibility, have interests in this operational environment. The importance of their initial assessment comes from determining possible enemy and third-party conditions shared between COCOMs, and the potential to coordinate for resources during the development and execution of COAs.

Department of Defense: During OEA, the representatives from the OSD and JCS assess the impact that National Command Authority

---

[58] JP 5-0, IV-3

guidance has on the operational environment. This is accomplished by referencing direct guidance of the President and SECDEF through directives, or in referencing established documents, such as the National Security Strategy, Guidance for the Employment of Forces, and National Military Strategy. The representatives of the military services and guard forces assess the status of their respective organizations in the categories of doctrine, organization, training, materiel, leadership, personnel, and facilities, and can communicate between the service chiefs and the COCOMs to ensure the interests of the services are being voiced. DTRA[59] and MDA[60] assess the nature of weapons of mass destruction (WMD); nuclear, biological, chemical, and explosives (NBC-E), within the region, and can produce charts and diagrams of relevant organizations whose posses such weapons, as well as, identify vulnerable infrastructure which may create destructive collateral effects. DISA, DLA, DSCA, and DSS provide further support by assessing the nature of similar organizations within the region, and can provide assessments of the conditions of information systems, international security cooperatives, and logistical capabilities. The importance of their initial assessments can help establish a benchmark of organic defense capabilities within the region, and during the final phases of joint operations, can help determine what conditions need to be altered in order to achieve the desired end-state. A competent, efficient and legitimate defense force is important towards the overall stability of a nation, especially as it emerges from a period of chaos, and the DOD can help shape similar organizations within the operational environment to provide that stability.

Department of State: During OEA, DOS has numerous products of varying categories to help fully understand the conditions of the operational environment. The representatives from the DOA will need to develop a portfolio of charts and diagrams depicting the

---

[59] Defense Threat Reduction Agency. *About DTRA / SCC-WMD.* Accessed July 28, 2014. http://www.dtra.mil/About.aspx

[60] Missile Defense Agency. *About Us.* Accessed July 28, 2014. http://www.mda.mil/about/about.html

status of agricultural production in the region, as well as, terrain and weather analysis in regards to their impact on yields. The DOC will bring forth information regarding the nature of commercial interests that have local, national, and international presence, including how the markets of the operational environment impact the way of life for its communities. DOEN can provide demographic assessments on the educational level of citizenry, and how the academic institutions operate within their systems. DHS and DOJ could provide evaluations on the efficiency and methods of police forces and legal systems which impact stability and legitimacy towards local governing bodies. DHHS can chart the locations and capabilities of various hospitals and other public health apparatuses, and how they impact the overall health of their various districts, whereas, representatives from HUD can determine the quality of living of communities within the operational environment, and assess how the conditions in which they live impact living standards. The DOI can provide lists of culturally sensitive or protected natural and manmade sites and parks, and assess how their importance plays into the perceptions of populations. DOL and Transportation reps will be able to provide demographics on the labor force of the operational environment, assessments on the infrastructure supporting the movement of people and goods, and how they tie into the economic health of the region. Members from the Department of the Treasury are capable of assessing how local governments fund programs, how loans and interest rates are handled, and how the management, printing, and distribution of currency is controlled. Finally, the VA can assess how government, private organizations, and communities care for its citizens during and after military service to their country, and what if any failure to do so disenfranchises them. The information gathered by the DOS during peacetime operations for the OEA will assist in properly assessing the nature of non-military conditions of the operational environment, and will provide joint staff and the EBB the requisite information necessary for shaping conditions.

National Intelligence Agencies: Not only can they support joint staff through the collection of various forms of intelligence gathering disciplines: Human, Geospatial, Measurement and Signature, Open Source, Signals, Technical, and Imagery,[61] [62] but can provide assessments on the presence and capabilities of other intelligence agencies operating within the operational environment. Evaluations of regional intelligence gathering activities will be necessary in order to determine how they impact the ability of a local government to govern effectively in the presence of internal and external threats, and where if possible the joint force and interagency organizations can shape them.

Other Organizations: While the attendance of some third-party organizations can limit what is able to be discussed during EBB and joint staff working groups the presence of other organizations within the operational environment can have an effect upon military operations. NGOs, like the Red Cross and World Bank Group, have operations throughout the world, and if present can provide further insight and guidance into conditions of the operational environment. IGOs, like the UN and NATO, may have information and resources which could be tapped during COA development, and knowledge of their status in the region may prove beneficial to the EBB. These organizations, however, have their own interests which they will seek to achieve that may help or hinder joint force efforts towards achieving the desired end-state. Regardless, IGOs and NGOs may be operating within the operational environment, and that mere presence adds another variable which needs to be tracked. If representatives are able to provide information to the EBB on their operations, and potentially garner their support, they may provide additional means during execution of joint force operations.

Foreign Elements: The inclusion of certain foreign representatives, much like certain IGOs and NGOs, can limit the nature of discussion within the EBB due the sensitivity of joint force

---

[61] Intelligence.GOV. Data *Gathering.* Accessed July 28, 2014. http://www.intelligence.gov/mission/data-gathering.html
[62] Federal Bureau of Investigations. *Intelligence Collection Disciplines.* Accessed July 28, 2014. http://www.fbi.gov/about-us/intelligence/disciplines

operations; however, they also bring with them numerous advantages. The presence of allied force liaisons means that they can voice the interests of their nations within the EBB, and the United States can attempt to alleviate certain concerns through understanding their interests within the operational environment. Temporary partner nations add to the overall pool of means available to the joint force for planning and execution, and can provide relevant information about the operational environment if their nations have frequent dealings within the region. Host nation representatives provide current assessments on the conditions of their country in not only tangible terms, but also more intangible attributes of the reign, such as religious sensitivities, trust in local government, and culturally defined perspectives. If applicable, neutral foreign parties may be included should the nature of the operational environment benefit from their involvement. These foreign entities can bring to the EBB not only the international perspective necessary to gauge how the military aspect of our foreign policy is perceived abroad, but can assist in coordinating for the capabilities of other nations towards the execution of COAs.

The preceding examples by no means encompass the entirety of what these organizations could produce for the OEA, and will require greater analysis from people more knowledgeable about these particular sectors' activities in order for the COCOM to fully benefit from their involvement during the JOPP. Regardless, once the initial collection and production of data for the OEA is complete the second step of the OEA can begin.

Step Two: Mission Analysis

At the beginning of mission analysis the joint staff will review national level strategic guidance, multinational guidance, and the CCDR's initial planning guidance in order to "analyze the operational approach to gain an appreciation for the commander's understanding and visualization."[63] This will allow the staff to begin developing the

---

[63] JP 5-0, IV-7

necessary facts and estimates, coupled with the data gathered during planning initiation, and produce the joint force mission statement. Concurrent to these developments the joint staff will deliver higher level guidance, and their current assessments, to the EBB.

During the second step of the OEA the board members compile their initial findings from the first step and present it to the group. They begin by stating the initial conditions of their respective sectors based on the seven universal conditions of the operational environment: *desired end-state, time, enemy conditions, third party conditions, collateral conditions, environmental conditions,* and *friendly conditions.* While presentations are being made two things are also occurring. First, other board members are taking notes of certain stated conditions they feel may also impact the conditions of their sectors. Second, the EBB's scribes are taking notes of all stated information, by conditions and sector, for future reference. As an example of this we will utilize the agricultural sector, being briefed by DOA representatives, on how their products could be utilized to define the initial conditions of a operational environment.

Desired end-state: Agricultural production will need to focus on legitimate forms of staple crops and livestock, and assessments of illicit crop production detail the level to which the current status of agriculture in the operational environment differs from that of the desired end-state.

Time: Seasonal weather patterns, crop maturity rates, soil richness, and agricultural infrastructure affect the planting, harvesting, and yield of crops, and based on desired ends the duration it takes to achieve a certain level of consistency and reliability in agricultural production will need to be accounted for during planning.

Enemy Conditions: Illicit crop production is influenced by belligerent organizations in certain regions of the operational environment, and they provide monetary incentives to farmers to continue production of those illicit crops.

Third Party Conditions: Foreign investors have been providing low-interests loans to local farmers for machinery designed to increase the yield of crops. Additionally, numerous international NGOs have been donating dairy cows to the farmers to communities increasing the volume of dairy products entering into local markets.

Collateral Conditions: Agricultural production accounts for the majority of the gross domestic product of the region, and the majority of families living in rural communities participate in some form of agricultural activity. We know that local communities prefer to conduct legitimate business will local farmers, and will avoid dealings with farmers producing drug crops.

Environmental Conditions: Certain regions of the operational environment have annual rainfall, water tables, soil pH levels, and soil richness/consistency able to support the production of certain types of crops up to an expected level of yield. Based on aforementioned information, diagrams depicting the viability of supporting certain types of crops may be portrayed. Additionally, through a depiction of the status of natural vegetation and access to water, the viability of raising livestock can be shown.

Friendly Conditions: DOA can contract the support of agricultural advisors to assist in local agricultural activities. Military veterinarians can help diagnose and vaccinate livestock to improve their health and productivity. NGOs and IGOs, currently active in the operational environment, may be able to coordinate with COCOM to achieve some unity of effort.

These few examples are by no means the extent of what the representatives of the DOA could brief, but are only meant to highlight how their particular sector can contribute information to each condition of the operational environment. As previously stated, while the scribes are making note of these identified conditions the other members of the EBB are starting to indentify links between the agricultural sector and their own. The DOC would take note of how the farmers are receiving monetary incentive from belligerent organizations, and that the dairy products from donated cattle are entering the local markets. DOL members would immediately indentify the importance that agriculture plays on the region's working class adults, and the COCOM reps can identify the DOA's potential need for veterinarians and determine where such support may be pulled. The identification of these linkages leads us into the next part of the OEA's mission analysis step.

Linking the identified conditions of the operational environment is an essential part of the process, because it helps us determine what potential STO effects may be created when we attempt to apply means to change those initial conditions. When altering the initial conditions into the required conditions, necessary for the desired end-state, a resulting cascade of effects may ripple throughout the various systems of the operational environment dependent on how it was accomplished. Through identifying the links between these initial conditions at this early phase we can begin to determine how cascading effects may function, and therefore provide guidance during the COA development phase of the JOPP to help promote positive, or mitigate negative, STO effects.

One possible way in which to illustrate the linkages is through a linkage diagram in which the universal conditions are juxtaposed to this operational environment's specific conditions described by the representatives. On the example linkage diagram (Figure 4), we can see a depiction of the information portrayed during the DOA brief. As each pair of representatives finishes briefing their piece, the EBB will have numerous linkage diagrams it will need to begin connecting to each other. Members that were able to make note of specific conditions of that operational environment that were mutually applicable to their sector can begin the process of coalescing all the diagrams into a single product. For example, one of the COCOM representatives can link their veterinary service personnel, falling under the friendly capabilities of their link diagram, to the livestock conditions of the DOA's diagram. Once all the link diagrams have themselves been linked then the EBB can begin to determine how to

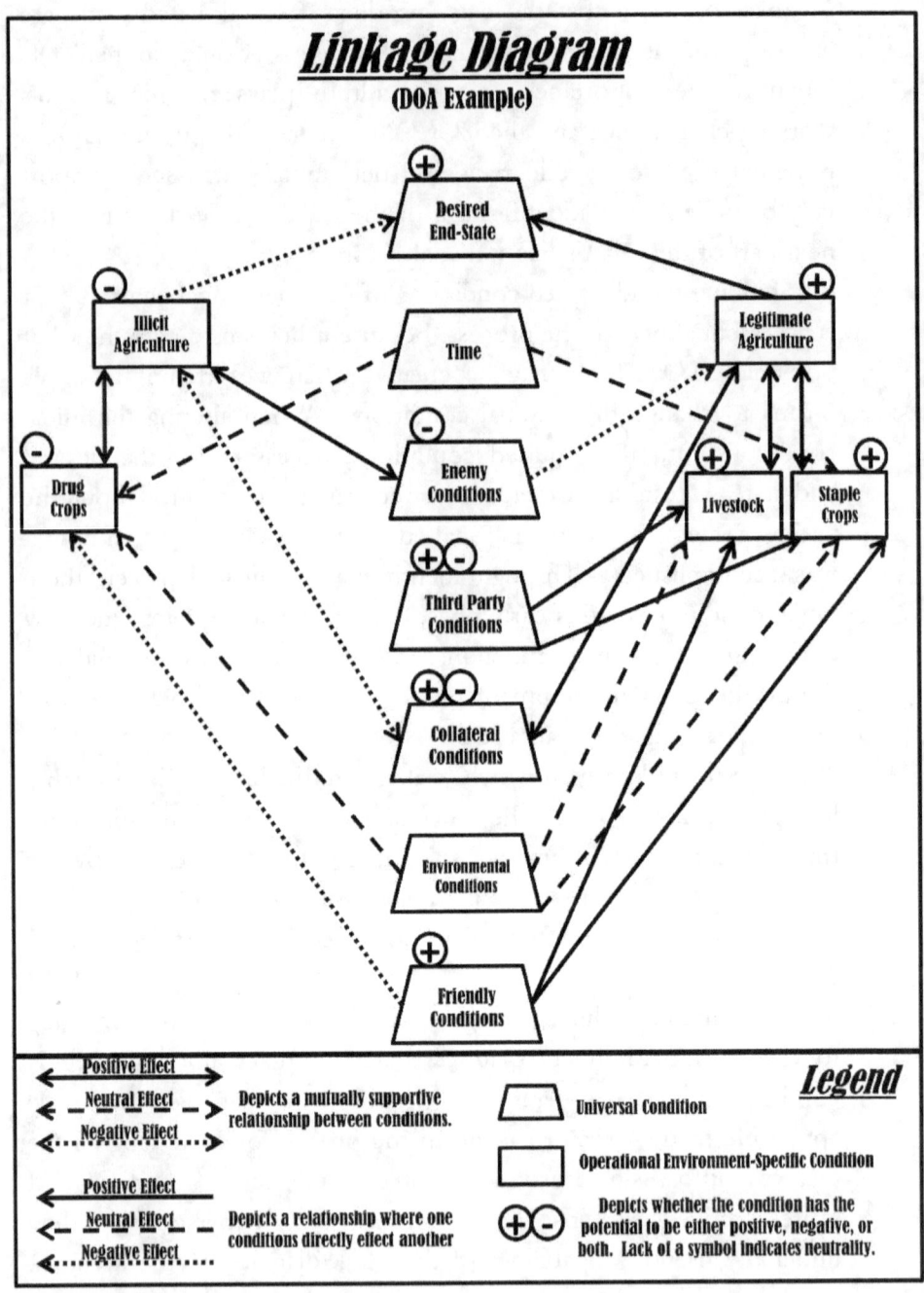

FIGURE 4

shape those conditions.

There are conditions within operational environment that support the desired end-state and will need to be promoted. Conversely, there are negative conditions which negatively impact the desired ends and will need to be negated. Utilizing the DOA example, in order to achieve the desired end-state we need to promote the positive effects of legitimate agriculture while negating the negative effects of illicit agriculture. The benefit of the linkage diagram is that we can see how those conditions themselves are negatively or positively affected, and where promotion or negation of linkages will be needed. In order to promote a strong legitimate agriculture we see that we need to combat the negative influence of the enemy, and promote the mutually supportive relationships between the markets of the local communities, the condition of livestock, and the condition of staple crops. If we continue further down the chain we can see that the condition of third party organizations and friendly capabilities can, and do, have a positive effect on livestock and staple crops; a connection that needs to be promoted. Similarly, we can analyze the linkage chain for illicit agriculture, and make a determination on which links to negate and which to promote.

The complexity of the operational environment becomes apparent when the EBB begins to analyze those linkages between multiple sectors of interest, and how the cascade of effects impacts the system. When the COCOM promotes the linkage between its veterinarian capabilities and the livestock of the communities, described by the DOA link diagram, it positively impacts legitimate agriculture which in turn positively impacts collateral conditions. Those collateral conditions have a negative effect on illicit agriculture which, as a result, weakens the positive connection between illicit agriculture and the enemy. The economic benefit denied to the belligerent organizations could weaken their impact in other sectors of the operational environment to which they produce negative effects, such as combating friendly forces or bribing local officials. A cascade of effects has rippled throughout the operational environment, and that cascade was first created by simply vaccinating cattle. In the end, what is developed is a detailed Operational Environment Link Diagram (OELD), which provides guidance on where to employ means to negate or promote linkages. It will be possible to shape that environment towards the desired end-state as positive conditions are strengthened and negative conditions are atrophied.

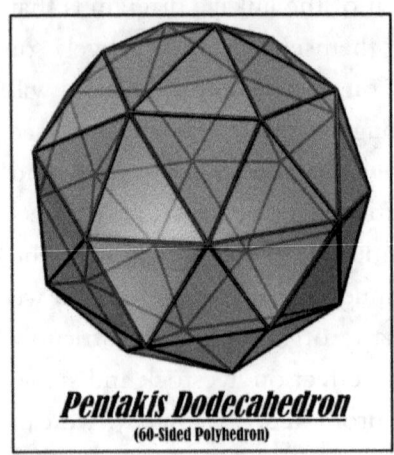

Pentakis Dodecahedron
(60-Sided Polyhedron)

FIGURE 5

Another way to visual these complex series of linkages is to imagine a polyhedron (Figure 5)[64] whose faces, or sides, represent an individual sector of the operational environment. The DOA link diagram would encompass a single face of that object complete with its internal links. The conditions displayed on that diagram which are linked to other conditions present in other sectors; i.e. other faces, would have a line that stretches through the inside of the polyhedron to connect those other conditions; complete with their own set of internal and external linkages. The object would look like a nervous or circulatory system which, in essence, would be representative of the conditions of the operational environment. When an effect is created upon one condition on one of the faces its effects reverberate throughout the linkages affecting the entirety of the object. When linkages are negated then the reverberations do not carry through to other conditions, but when the link is promoted the reverberations are much stronger. Once all the necessary links have been negated or promoted within the object then each successive application of effects strengthen the positive conditions and weaken the negative

---

[64] Wikipedia, Pentakis Dodecahedron. Accessed July 30, 2014. http://en.wikipedia.org/wiki/Pentakis_dodecahedron#

ones, slowly shaping the object towards the desired end-state.

With an understanding of the operational environment to this level of detail the EBB can then participate in the COA develop step of the JOPP, and begin assessing how the COAs developed by the joint staff impact achievement of the desired end-state.

Step Three: COA Development

When the joint staff conducts COA development they are producing plans which are tentative in nature, and subject to change based on the needs of the operational environment. "Each COA describes, in broad but clear terms, what is to be done throughout the campaign or operations the size of forces deemed necessary, and time in which joint force capabilities need to be brought to bear."[65] The intent is to give the commander a number of options in which to execute military operations in order to achieve the *military end state*.[66] Once the joint staff has completed the development of COAs, and is confident to carry them onto the next step, they will have produced plans that provide a concept of the operations.

Each COA typically will constitute an operational concept and provide a narrative and sketch that include the following: objectives, key tasks, major capabilities required, task organization, main and supporting efforts, sustainment concept, deployment concept, strategic communication supporting themes, identification of reserve, and identification of required supporting interagency tasks.[67]

Unlike the standard process of the JOPP, this new process includes the vetting of those COAs through the EBB prior to briefing them to the CCDR. The board will utilize its consolidated link diagram of the operational environment, the OELD, in order to determine the viability of those COAs to achieve the desired end-state. From this joint staff / EBB engagement we are seeking to

---

[65] JP 5-0, IV-18
[66] JP 5-0, IV-17
[67] JP 5-0, IV-18 & IV-19

achieve four things which improve the COAs ability to achieve that end-state.

First, the COAs will suggest the utilization of various means in order to achieve certain effects, and the EBB will be charged with assessing as to whether or not those means utilized will actually achieve the effects they claim. Second, utilizing the OELD, the EBB will determine how the creation of effects against certain conditions will cascade throughout the operational environment, and identify those positive and negative STO effects. Third, understanding how the proposed COAs will affect the conditions within the operational environment if negative effects are unintentionally created or if positive effects are not effectively produced they will provide guidance to alternative means to be utilized. Additionally, if alternatives are not possible, they will provide guidance on how to mitigate the negative attributes of STO effects, and suggest additions to the COA to produce effects against other conditions that hadn't been engaged. Fourth, once the plans have been determined to support the desired end-state of the operational environment the joint staff can work through the EBB in order to begin the process of coordinating for means outside of the COCOM's organic capabilities.

Once this guidance has been provided to the joint staff they return to their shops to make the appropriate changes to the COAs. After adjusted, the joint staff and the EBB will brief the COAs to the CCDR, component commanders, and special staff (Figure 6). The joint staff describes the concept of operations for each COA, by phase, and the EBB details the nature of effects produced during those operations. By the end of the brief, the CCDR will provide guidance to the joint staff based on new information or guidance coming from the National Command Authority. This will allow them to update their facts and estimates, and prepare for the analysis step of the JOPP.

EFFECTS-BASED BOARD LAYOUT
(PACOM Example)

MILITARY

DISA	DLA	DSCA	DSS	DTRA	MDA	IGO/NGO	IGO/NGO	IGO/NGO	AMERICAN RED CROSS
OSD	JCS	ARMY	NAVY	MARINES	AIR FORCE	COAST GUARD	NATNL GUARD	IGO/NGO	IGO/NGO
USNORTHCOM	USSOUTHCOM	USEUCOM	USAFRICOM	USCENTCOM	USSOCOM	USTRANSCOM	USNORTHCOM	USCYBERCOM	USSTRATCOM

OTHERS

NON-MILITARY

USAID	NATO	UN	WORLD BANK	CONGRESS LNO	EXECUTIVE LNO	JUDICIAL LNO	CIA	FBI
DOJ	DOI	DOT	TREASURY	VA	DIA	NSA	NGIA	NRO
OSS	DOA	DOC	DOED	DOE	DHHS	DHS	HUD	DOI

FOREIGN LNOs

HOST NATION (JAPAN)	CONGRESS (JAPAN)	PARTNER (THAILAND)	ALLY (KOREA)
HOST NATION (JAPAN)	HOST NATION (JAPAN)	PARTNER (THAILAND)	ALLY (KOREA)
HOST NATION (JAPAN)	HOST NATION (JAPAN)	PARTNER (PHILIPPINES)	ALLY (AUSTRALIA)
HOST NATION (JAPAN)	HOST NATION (JAPAN)	PARTNER (PHILIPPINES)	ALLY (AUSTRALIA)
HOST NATION (JAPAN)	HOST NATION (JAPAN)	PARTNER (VIETNAM)	ALLY (UK)
HOST NATION (JAPAN)	HOST NATION (JAPAN)	PARTNER (VIETNAM)	ALLY (UK)

COCOM/JTF ELEMENT

CHAPLAIN	J6	JIACG	GROUND COMPONENT
INSPECTOR GENERAL	J5	STAFF JUDGE ADVOCATE	AIR COMPONENT
FAO	J4	PUBLIC AFFAIRS	MARITIME COMPONENT
J9	J3	SENIOR ENLISTED LEADER	SPECIAL OPS COMPONENT
J8	J2	DEPUTY CHIEF OF STAFF	DEPUTY PACOM COMMANDER
J7	J1	CHIEF OF STAFF	PACOM COMMANDER

Analog Floor Display of Operational Environment

Digital Wall Display of Operational Environment

SCRIBE	SCRIBE	SCRIBE	SCRIBE	Display Operator

FIGURE 6

Step Four: COA Analysis

The analysis step of the JOPP focuses on wargaming COAs against enemy MLCOAs and MDCOAs in order to ensure joint staff planning is effectively accounting for expected scenarios and outcomes. "Wargaming is a conscious attempt to visualize the flow of the operation, given joint force strengths and dispositions, adversary capabilities and possible COAs, the [operational approach], and other aspects of the operational environment."[68]   At the conclusion the joint staff should have a relatively confident assessment that their COAs are both feasible and acceptable. To support this analysis the EBB assesses actions executed during wargaming against the OELD to ensure the cascade of effects supports the overall commander's intent and the desired end-state.

While the joint staff develops potential decision points, determines commander evaluation criteria, assesses potential COA variations, refines COAs, and revises their estimates[69] the EBB has the opportunity to reassess the validity of the OELD. As the COAs are wargamed naturally new information about the operational environment may be produced to which were not completely indentified during the OEA at the beginning of the JOPP. When new information is processed through the OELD, determining which initial conditions have been changed or if new conditions have to be incorporated, it will have an impact on the assessment that the OELD provides. Something as simple as a new third-party actor appearing within the operational environment can change the nature in which effects cascade throughout it. If new information doesn't fit within the existing design of the OELD, meaning already defined conditions explain for this new information, then the EBB will need to refine its own internal linkages to account for what is now new initial conditions.

With refined COAs and an updated OELD, the joint staff and EBB will then brief the CCDR on the outcomes of the analysis.

---

[68] JP 5-0, IV-27
[69] JP 5-0, IV-28

Once approved by the commander, the staff and board are coming towards the end of this lengthy and complex process.

Step Five: COA Comparison

During the COA comparison step of the JOPP the purpose of the joint staff is to, "identify and recommend the COA that has the highest probability of success against the enemy COA that is of the most concern to the commander."[70]   In the end, the joint staff is attempting to execute a plan that achieves the objectives of the military end-state which is nested with, but not directly similar to, the desired end-state of the operational environment. This is necessary in order to satisfy the commander's intent, but there are non-military aspects not represented in the military end-state that need to be accounted for. That is why the EBB, with its OELD, still has an important part even this late in the process.

The OELD is built around shaping the conditions of the operational environment towards the desired end-state, and at this final step prior to approval it can have a final say before the COCOM and supporting agencies begin movement towards execution. The EBB, when bumping the COAs presented against the OELD, provide an authoritative thumbs-up to the CCDR that they do indeed support the desired end-state. Additionally, with the nature of the EBB containing so many subject matter experts in all the sectors necessary to bring about the desired end-state they can provide an assessment of the associated costs that the COAs will produce as a result of execution. Essentially putting a best-guess estimate price-tag to which the CCDR and the National Command Authority will have to budget.

After a final vetting through the EBB, the COAs that the joint staff presents to the CCDR not only meet with the desired military end-state, but also satisfy the overall desired end-state of the operational environment based on the best assessment of that environment possible; the OELD. This step finishes with the

---

[70] JP 5-0, IV 36

commander providing last-minute corrections to any outstanding discrepancies that are discovered, and selects a COA for which the joint staff will then begin preparations for the publication of the plan.

Step Six: COA Approval

Prior to final approval and publication, the joint staff is also producing that last few additions necessary for the deployment of forces and resources. One addition being the Time-Phased Force and Deployment Data (TPFDD) which is the "time-phased force data, non-unit cargo and personnel data, and movement data for the operation plan or operation order or ongoing rotation of forces."[71] This includes identifying which types of military organizations and resources are required to support the final plan, and how to transport those elements to the operational environment.

EBB contributions to the final plan will be in producing appendixes to which give strategic guidance towards the employment of means. This is accomplished by providing two sets of products. The first product is strategic level guidance based on the OELD which describes critical activities that need to be undertaken and how those activities impact the environment. It is basically a simplified, bullet point spreadsheet of those linkages identified in the OELD as needed to either be promoted or negated in order to achieve the desired end-state. They state, in a simple narrative, broadly defined activities that can or should be taken, how those actions create direct and STO effects within the operational environment, and finally how that cascade of effects supports the desired end-state. The second product is the refined OEA documents, from the planning initiation and mission analysis steps of the JOPP, as an additional appendix to the final operation plan for use by subordinate elements.

The intent is that these products can be disseminated down to the lowest operational and tactical level of organizations in order to support their own development of local operation orders. They can be provided to squad leaders, engagement teams, foreign partners,

---

[71] JP 1-02, 268

and local governing authorities in order to inform them how their actions could impact the overall mission of the joint force. Through its broad descriptions of what activities support the desired end-state it helps in the execution of mission command by giving forces the ability to apply strategic effects upon tactical level linkages. This has effectively empowered the *strategic corporal*[72] concept through providing junior leaders or actors the ability to actively and knowingly shape conditions towards the desired end-state. The final COA, with all its accoutrement, will pass through the CCDR for final approval and then published.

Step Seven: Plan/Order Development

During the publication of what is now an official operations plan or order, the EBB's participation within the JOPP in now complete. This, however, does not mean that they are no longer supporting efforts to shape conditions within the operational environment. Two things after the dissemination of plans, and throughout execution of operations, occur that the EBB will conduct.

First, is the standard peacetime affair of assessing the environment of the COCOM's area of responsibility, and updating their continuity of assessments and diagrams for possible future deliberate and crisis action plans. By continuously updating their documents as time progresses will ensure that when the JOPP begins again, possibly in a new operational environment, that they will have the products necessary for beginning the OEA during the planning initiation step. Just because the COCOM has invested its efforts into the current engagement doesn't mean that they have relinquished their responsibility to react to a new issue elsewhere, and the EBB needs to be prepared for that eventuality.

Second, the current operational environment's initial conditions will change through both intended applications of effects, as well as,

---

[72] Liddy, Lynda MAJ. "The Strategic Corporal: Some Requirements in Training and Education." *Australian Army Journal* Volume II, Number 2. Accessed August 1, 2014. http://smallwarsjournal.com/documents/liddy.pdf, 140

the effects of known and unknown conditions acting upon that environment. The EBB will need to continue to reassess whether the OELD, and the products disseminated based on it, are still applicable as the environment changes. If all potential conditions had been identified and account for then the OELD should not change, but naturally we don't have an omnipotent view of the world around us and small, unforeseen conditions may be presented during operations that change the way effects cascade. If a new condition is identified then the OELD is updated, and if applicable, new products are disseminated down the chain.

VII
CONCLUSION

There is not a more important time to achieve success than preparation prior to execution of operations, and through understanding the initial conditions of the operational environment, as well as their relationships, it will provide the structure necessary for which to develop COAs. In order to understand the operational environment to such a level we need a board of members whose collective knowledge is representative of the desired end-state we are trying to achieve; namely legitimate and stable governments. From this board we can develop a realization of the operational environment that is as complete as possible, and will be able to guide the development of plans. It provides an effects-based approach to the development of COAs, because it not only develops a detailed and holistic comprehension of the operational environment, it also helps determine how certain military and non-military actions will create certain effects and shape the conditions of that environment. This allows for a whole of government approach to the selection of various elements of national power, because through the EBB we can determine if the same desired effects can also be achieved through different means.

During a "TED Talks" speaking session, retired General Stanley McChrystal spoke about a need to share information with not only those that need to know that information, but to everyone possible. "Information is only of value if you give it to people who have the ability to do something with it. The fact that I know something has zero value if I am not the person who can actually make something better because of it... We changed the idea of information, instead of *knowledge is power*, to one where *sharing is power*."[73] Based on his perspective, military planners developing COAs without the support of a board, such as the EBB, are coordinating sets of actions against conditions they may not fully understand. They have a *need to know* the inner-workings of the operational environment, those conditions and their relationships, in order to pair desired effects with available means. The EBB is about sharing an understanding of the operational environment to the degree to which the joint staff of the COCOM can develop COAs that can achieve the desired end-state. Beyond that they provide guidance to the CCDR on the potential effects that can arise when particular actions are taken, and can provide alternative COAs based on available means.

The impact that military operations have on United States foreign policy, and its national interests, is a critical one. The nature of the operational environment is of a complex system of systems in which conditions and their relationships determine the effects of actions that are applied to it. There are more than just enemy and friendly conditions at play, and something as simple as soil consistency of a particular region can help or hinder military and non-military efforts to shape the conditions of that environment. If our desired end-state for military operations is the establishment of legitimate civil governments and stability for their citizenry than the EBB, which represents a microcosm of our own legitimate government and stable society, will provide the necessary guidance for the develop of COAs needed to shape conditions required of that end-state.

---

[73] McChrystal, Stanley GEN (USA). *Stanley McChrystal: The military case for sharing knowledge.* Accessed July 05, 2014.
https://www.youtube.com/watch?v=9jRkACywckE&index=2&list=FLTIUFrlaW-2-d9V5NjNx8LQ 4:42

A
LIST OF REFERENCES

Afghanistan Ministry of Counter Narcotics & United Nations Office on Drugs and Crime. *Afghanistan Opium Survey 2013*. Accessed 04 July, 2014. http://www.unodc.org/documents/crop-monitoring/Afghanistan/Afghan_report_Summary_Findings_2013.pdf

Appleman, Roy E. LTC (USA). *Disaster in Korea.* College Station, TX; Texas A&M, 1989

Bergen, Perter, "How Petraeus changed the U.S. military" *CNN*, Accessed June 23,2014. http://www.cnn.com/2012/11/10/opinion/bergen-petraeus-legacy/.

Clark, Wesley K. GEN (USA). *Waging Modern War.* New York, NY; PublicAffairs, 2001

Coalition Provisional Authority, *Coalition Provisional Authority Order Number 2*. Accessed August 02, 2014. http://www.casi.org.uk/info/cpa/030523-CPA-Order2.pdf

Cohen, Eliot A. & John Gooch. *Military Misfortunes.* New York, NY; Free Press, 2006

Cordesman, Anthony H. *The Lessons and Non-Lessons of the Air and Missile Campaign in Kosovo.* Westport, CT; Praeger Publishing, 2001

Correll, John T. "The Assault on EBO." *AIR FORCE Magazine*. Arlington, VA; Air Force Association, January 2013

Defense Threat Reduction Agency. *About DTRA / SCC-WMD*. Accessed July 28, 2014. http://www.dtra.mil/About.aspx

Department of the Army. *Field Manual 3-60: Targeting*. Washington, D.C.: Government Printing Office, 2010

Department of Defense. *Directive 2311.01E: DoD Law of War Program*. Accessed 28 June, 2014. http://www.dtic.mil/whs/directives/corres/pdf/231101e.pdf

Deptula, David A. BG (USAF). *Effects-Based Operations: Change in the Nature of Warfare*. Arlington, VA; Aerospace Education Foundation, 2001

Federal Bureau of Investigation. *Intelligence Collection Disciplines*. Accessed July 28, 2014. http://www.fbi.gov/about-us/intelligence/disciplines

Gibbs, David N. "Afghanistan: The Soviet Invasion Retrospect" *International Politics*. Tucson, AZ; University of Arizona, 2000

Gordon, Trainor R. & Bernard E. Trainor GEN (USA). *The Generals' War*. New York, NY; Back Bay Books, 1995

Hannan, Michael J. LCDR (USN). *Operational Net Assessment: A Framework for Social Network Analysis*. Accessed May 18, 2014. http://www.au.af.mil/info-ops/iosphere/iosphere_fall05_hannan.pdf

Intelligence.GOV. *Data Gathering*. Accessed July 28, 2014. http://www.intelligence.gov/mission/data-gathering.html

Jobbagy, Zoltan. "Effects-based Operations and the Problem of Causality." *Joint Forces Quarterly*. Washington, D.C.; NDU Press, issue 46, 3rd quarter 2007

Joint Staff, *Joint Publication 1: Doctrine for the Armed Forces of the United States*. Washington, D.C.; Government Printing Office, 2013

Joint Staff, *Joint Publication 1-02: Department of Defense Dictionary of Military and Associated Terms.* Washington, D.C.; Government Printing Office, 2014

Joint Staff, *Joint Publication 2-01.3: Joint Intelligence Preparation of the Operational Environment.* Washington, D.C.; Government Printing Office, 2009

Joint Staff. *Joint Publication 5-0: Joint Operation Planning.* Washington, D.C.; Government Printing Office, 2011

Joint Warfighting Center. *Commander's Handbook for an Effects-Based Approach to Joint Operations.* Washington, D.C.; Government Printing Office, 2006

Juno Beach Centre. *The Dieppe Raid.* Accessed June 29, 2014. http://www.junobeach.org/canada-in-wwii/articles/the-dieppe-raid/

Liddy, Lynda MAJ. "The Strategic Corporal: Some Requirements in Training and Education." *Australian Army Journal* Volume II, Number 2. Accessed August 1, 2014. http://smallwarsjournal.com/documents/liddy.pdf

Matthews, Matt M. *We Were Caught Unprepared: The 2006 Hezbollah-Israeli War.* Fort Leavenworth, KS; Combat Studies Institute Press, 2008

Mattis, James N. GEN (USMC) "USJFCOM Commander's Guidance for Effects-based Operations." *Joint Forces Quarterly.* Washington, D.C.; NDU Press, issue 51, 4th quarter 2008

McChrystal, Stanley GEN (USA). *Stanley McChrystal: The military case for sharing knowledge.* Accessed July 05, 2014. https://www.youtube.com/watch?v=9jRkACywckE&index=2&list=FLTIUFrlaW-2-d9V5NjNx8LQ

Missile Defense Agency. *About Us.* Accessed July 28, 2014. http://www.mda.mil/about/about.html

Moorehead, Alan. *Gallipoli.* Harper, NY; The Nautical & Aviation Publishing Company of America, 1956

Murray, Williamson. "Triumph of Operation Torch" *World War II Magazine*. Leesburg, VI; Weider History Group 2002

Obama, Barack H. *National Security Strategy*. Washington, D.C.; Government Printing Office, 2010

Sawyer, Ralph D. *Sun Tzu: Art of War.* Boulder, CO; Westview Press, 1994

Smith, Edward A. *Effects Based Operations: Applying Network Centric Warfare in Peace, Crisis, and War.* Washington, D.C.; CCRP Press, 2002

Wade, Norman W. *The Joint Forces Operations and Doctrine: SMARTbook 3rd Edition*. Lakeland, FL: The Lightning Press, 2012

Wikipedia, Pentakis Dodecahedron. Accessed July 30, 2014. http://en.wikipedia.org/wiki/Pentakis_dodecahedron#

B
LIST OF ACRONYMS

C2	Command and Control
CCDR	Combatant Commander
CCIR	Commander's Critical Information Requirements
CIA	Central Intelligence Agency
COA	Course of Action
COCOM	Combatant Command
COG	Center of Gravity
DA	Department of the Army
DAF	Department of the Air Force
DP	Decision Point
DHHS	Department of Health and Human Services
DHS	Department of Homeland Security
DIA	Defense Intelligence Agency
DIME	Diplomatic, Informational, Military and Economic
DISA	Defense Information Systems Agency
DLA	Defense Logistics Agency
DOA	Department of Agriculture

DOC	Department of Commerce
DOE	Department of Energy
DOED	Department of Education
DOI	Department of the Interior
DOJ	Department of Justice
DOL	Department of Labor
DON	Department of the Navy
DOT	Department of Transportation
DSCA	Defense Security Cooperation Agency
DSS	Defense Security Service
DTRA	Defense Threat Reduction Agency
EBA	Effects-Based Approach
EBB	Effects-Based Board
EBO	Effects-Based Operations
FBI	Federal Bureau of Investigation
FRAGO	Fragmentary Orders
HUD	Department of Housing and Urban Development
IADS	Integrated Air Defense System
IDF	Israeli Defense Force
IGO	Intergovernmental Organization
JCS	Joint Chiefs of Staff
JFC	Joint Force Commander
JIPOE	Joint Intelligence Preparation of the Operational Environment
JOPP	Joint Operations Planning Process
KLA	Kosovo Liberation Army
LOAC	Law of Armed Conflict

LOW	Law of War
MDA	Missile Defense Agency
MDCOA	Most Dangerous Course of Action
MLCOA	Most Likely Course of Action
MOOTW	Military Operations Other Than War
NATO	North Atlantic Treaty Organization
NBC-E	Nuclear, Biological, Chemical, and Explosives
NGB	National Guard Bureau
NGIA	National Geospatial Intelligence Agency
NGO	Non-Governmental Organization
NKPA	North Korean People's Army
NRO	National Reconnaissance Office
NSA	National Security Agency
OEA	Operational Environment Assessment
OELD	Operational Environment Link Diagram
OIF	Operation Iraqi Freedom
ONA	Operational Net Assessment
OSD	Office of the Secretary of Defense
OSS	Office of the Secretary of State
PIR	Priority Intelligence Requirements
PMESII	Political, Military, Economic, Social, Information, and Infrastructure
PRT	Provincial Reconstruction Team
ROK	Republic of Korea
SACEUR	Supreme Allied Commander, Europe
SECDEF	Secretary of Defense

SES	Senior Executive Service
SOSA	System-of-System Analysis
STO	Second and Third-Order
TPFDD	Time-Phased Force and Deployment Data
UN	United Nations
USAFRICOM	United States Africa Command
USAID	United States Agency for International Development
USCENTCOM	United States Central Command
USCG	United States Coast Guard
USCYBERCOM	United States Cyber Command
USEUCOM	United States European Command
USJFCOM	United States Joint Force Command
USMC	United States Marine Corps
USNORTHCOM	United States Northern Command
USPACOM	United States Pacific Command
USSOCOM	United States Special Operations Command
USSOUTHCOM	United States Southern Command
USSTRATCOM	United States Strategic Command
USTRANSCOM	United States Transportation Command
VA	Department of Veteran Affairs
WMD	Weapons of Mass Destruction

C
ARTWORK OF DANNY HUYNH

http://www.artofdannyhuynh.com/

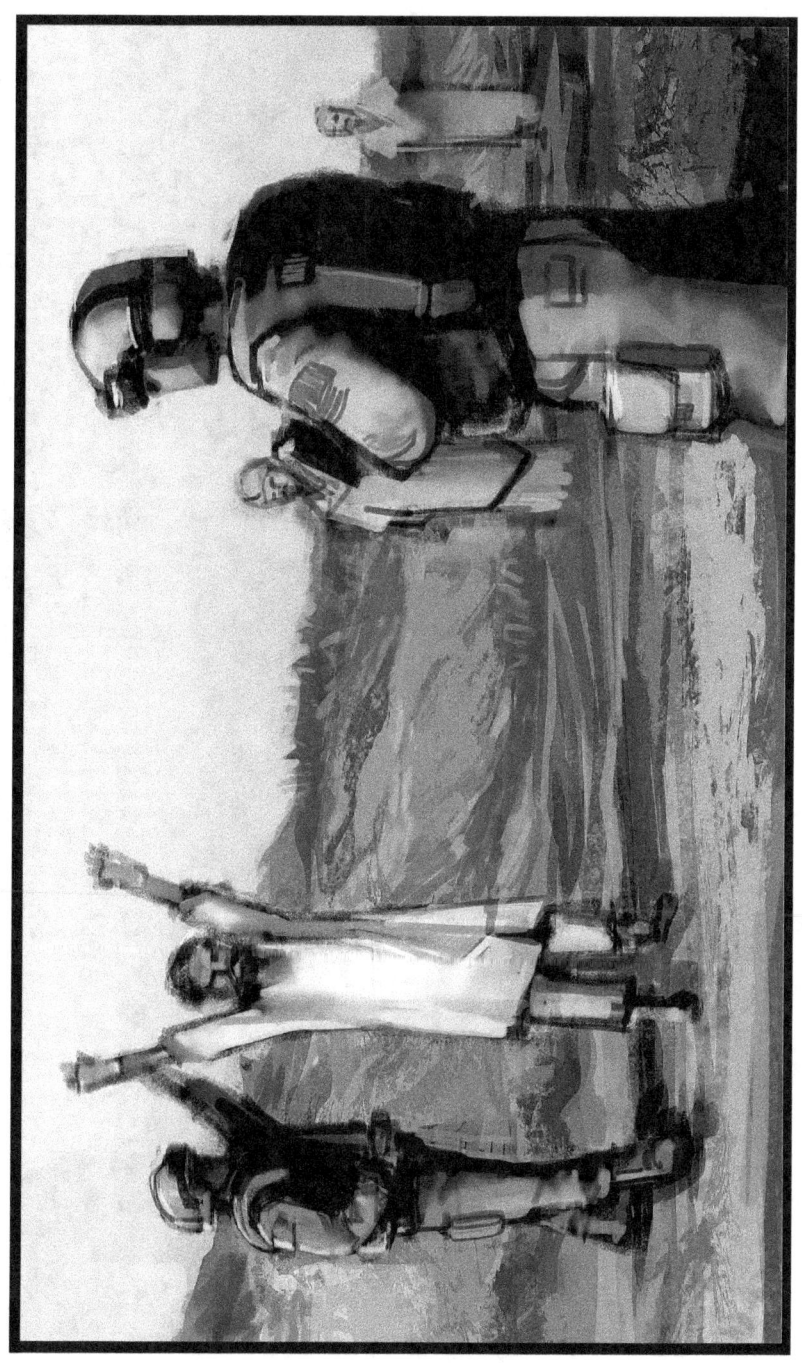

ABOUT THE AUTHOR

Colin Marcum holds a Bachelor of Arts in History, and minors in Military Science and Japanese, from Oregon State University. He also holds a Master of Arts in Military Studies from the American Military University. After serving four years as an Infantryman with the Oregon Army National Guard from 2005 to 2009, he received his commission as an active duty Field Artillery Officer in the United States Army. After completing Basic Officer Leader Course at Fort Sill, Oklahoma, he completed a three-year tour in the Republic of Korea before returning to Fort Sill. He now serves as the Assistant to the Director of Strategic Communications at the Fires Center of Excellence and Fort Sill at the rank of Captain. He is accompanied by his wife, Hillma, and daughter, Ellie.